DETERMINE YOUR SPECIFIC WEIGHT-LOSS CHALLENGE!

Check the statements that describe normal patterns for you.

_____ You always or usually skip breakfast.

_____ You feel compelled to eat when you are under stress, angry, bored, or excited.

_____ You are more hungry after you begin to eat than when you were before you started.

_____ You aren't sure what physical hunger feels like.

_____ You usually overeat when you're alone.

_____ You consume sixty percent or more of your daily calories in the evening.

_____ You snack frequently during the day.

_____ You take laxatives or diuretics after you eat.

_____ When you overeat one day, you try not to eat much the following day.

_____ You never feel hungry in the morning.

_____ There are certain foods that seem to give you comfort when you eat them.

_____ You have had bulemic episodes—binging followed by vomiting.

_____ You don't have a structured exercise program.

_____ You exercise more than one hour daily.

Your answers to this inventory and other questions inside the book will define your treatment method. Dr. Callaway's four-step personal inventory will target the most effective diet approach for _you_—based on your ideal weight range, dieting history, eating and exercise patterns, and current metabolic rate.

The Callaway Diet

Successful Permanent Weight Control for Starvers, Stuffers, and Skippers

C. Wayne Callaway, M.D.
with Catherine Whitney

BANTAM BOOKS
NEW YORK • TORONTO • LONDON • SYDNEY • AUCKLAND

THE CALLAWAY DIET

A Bantam Book
Bantam hardcover edition / May 1990
Bantam nonfiction paperback edition / March 1991

Grateful acknowledgment is made to McGraw-Hill Publishing Company for permission to reprint material from Geriatric Medicine *by Reubin Andres, Edwin L. Bierman, William R. Hazzard, eds., copyright © 1984.*

BANTAM NONFICTION *and the portrayal of a boxed "b" are trademarks of Bantam Books, a division of Bantam Doubleday Dell Publishing Group, Inc.*

Published simultaneously in the United States and Canada

Bantam Books are published by Bantam Books, a division of Bantam Doubleday Dell Publishing Group, Inc. Its trademark, consisting of the words "Bantam Books" and the portrayal of a rooster, is Registered in U.S. Patent and Trademark Office and in other countries. Marca Registrada. Bantam Books, 666 Fifth Avenue, New York, New York 10103.

PRINTED IN THE UNITED STATES OF AMERICA

OPM   0 9 8 7 6 5 4 3 2 1

TO ABE AND BETTY

Acknowledgments

Writing a book is not a solitary endeavor. This one could not have been written without the support of many people. In particular, I would like to express appreciation to my writing collaborator, Catherine Whitney, who was sensitive to the human problems of chronic dieters and shared my desire to construct a program that would make a difference in their lives. I also want to thank Alexandra Penney, the editor at Bantam whose vision made this book possible, and Coleen O'Shea, whose editing skill added immeasurably to the finished product. The efforts of my agents, Jonna Lynne Cullen and Jane Dystel, were essential to this book becoming a reality.

My staff gave generously of their time and energy during the time I was writing the book. In particular, I am grateful for the major contribution of Kristine Mehring, whose creative meal plans and recipes make the diet plans both healthy and exciting.

Research is never a one-man show, and my work could never have evolved to its present state without the dedication and skill of the many men and women who have contributed to this field. My mentors and colleagues at the Mayo Clinic were instrumental in helping me form the foundations of this work. I am also thankful to George F. Cahill, of Harvard Medical School, with whom I had the privilege of working during two critical years of my scientific development, and whose studies of human starvation have profoundly affected my thinking.

My colleagues in the field have contributed to my life and work with their important research, their insights, and their support. I'd like to acknowledge the work of all who have contributed to the study of human obesity, in particular, Rubin Andres, Per Bjornthorp, Claude Bouchard, George A. Bray, Kelly D. Brownell, John P. Foreyt, M.R.C. Greenwood, Gail Harrison, Peter Herman, Jules Hirsch, Edward S. Horton, John G. Kral, Rudolph Leibel, Lewis Landsberg, Janet Polivy, Cheryl Rittenbaugh, Ethan A.H. Sims, Albert J. Stunkard, Theodore Van Itallie, Mei-Uih Yang, and J.B. Young. I am also grateful for the contributions that the younger colleagues who have studied or worked with me have made, in particular, Michael Albert, Rachel Ballard-Barbash, Pamela Gurnick, and Maria Rojeski. And I'd like to thank Cecelia Pemberton and Mary Hankey for their clinical support

Over the years, our work has been generously supported by many organizations, which have provided funding, sponsored public education programs, and developed a variety of forums for professionals and consumers. I especially appreciate the opportunities provided by the National Institutes of Health, the American Medical Association, the American Dietetics Association, and the National Dairy Council.

Special thanks to Louis M. Sheldahl, of the Veterans Administration Medical Center, for his studies on the benefits of exercise; and to Richard B. Stuart, for his work on behavior modification. And my deep appreciation to Kerry Tucker for his advice and assistance in generating media support for my work.

The value of those who have added to my personal life cannot be measured. I want them all to know how important they've been. In particular, I'm grateful to my parents, to my son, David, and especially to my wife and confidant, Maggie.

Finally, I want to thank the thousands of men and women who have been my patients during the past twenty years. Their spirit, honesty, and courage have been a constant inspiration to me and have made my work a joy.

Contents

A Message to the Reader:
Be a Part of the Research

The Callaway Diet represents groundbreaking research in human obesity, including the ways the body resists losing weight on low calorie diets, and how long-term weight control can be achieved. And the research continues with this book. My commitment is to new knowledge and further refinement of this unconventional diet approach—with the help of people like you.

As you will see when you read *The Callaway Diet*, I have based this program on my experience with thousands of men and women who struggle with weight control. Since individuals are unique in the way they respond to treatment, your input will make an important contribution to this work.

If you would like to contribute to the research project, answer the questions on the following four-part form. Fill out part 1 before you read the book. Fill out part 2 after you read the book. Part 3 is your agreement to become part of a study project designed to evaluate the experiences of people who follow the program. If you are selected to take part in the study, your identity and data will be held in confidentiality. Part 4 should be filled out if you are interested in setting up a support group of at least four people who will follow the program together and meet once a week for at least eight weeks. This is part of a system of support groups we are planning to set up during the next several years.

You may find it gratifying to know that you can play a role in helping others like yourself who may have nearly given up hope that they can get off the weight loss/weight gain treadmill. I thank you in advance for your valuable assistance.

—*C. Wayne Callaway, M.D.*

Research Data

(Name identification is optional, but be sure to supply it if you agree to be contacted at a later date.)

NAME_____

ADDRESS_____

CITY_____ STATE _____ ZIP_____

TELEPHONE_____

SEX (M) _____ (F) _____

AGE _____

EDUCATION
(a) advanced degree;
(b) graduated college;
(c) attended college;
(d) graduated high school;
(e) did not graduate high school.

PROFESSION_____

AVERAGE ANNUAL FAMILY INCOME
(a) over $50,000;
(b) $35,000–50,000;
(c) $20,000–35,000;
(d) under $20,000.

PART 1
(Answer These Questions *Before* You Read the Book.)

(Use a separate sheet of paper if you want to expand on any of your answers.)

DATE:_____

1. What are your attitudes about weight and dieting?

_____

_____

_____

Circle True (T) or False (F) for the following questions:

- If you eat less, you'll lose weight.   T   F
- Overeating happens for psychological reasons.   T   F
- People of normal weight have more control over food cravings.   T   F
- Being overweight prevents you from having the things you want in life.   T   F
- Thin people have better personal relationships than overweight people.   T   F
- Thin people are more successful than overweight people.   T   F
- Overweight people are less attractive than thin people.   T   F

2. Your current weight is _____. Your height is _____.

You believe that you are: ＿＿ underweight;
＿＿ normal weight; ＿＿ slightly overweight;
＿＿ moderately overweight; ＿＿ very
overweight.

3. At what age did you first gain excess weight? ＿
   Describe your life at that time (e.g., job, marital
   status, school, pregnancy, major life change, etc.)
   ＿＿＿＿＿＿＿＿＿＿＿＿＿＿＿＿＿＿＿＿＿
   ＿＿＿＿＿＿＿＿＿＿＿＿＿＿＿＿＿＿＿＿＿
   ＿＿＿＿＿＿＿＿＿＿＿＿＿＿＿＿＿＿＿＿＿

4. Check the items that are true for you:

   ＿＿ You have frequently dieted to lose weight.
   ＿＿ You have lost weight dieting in the past.
   ＿＿ You have used amphetamines.
   ＿＿ You have used over-the-counter diet pills.
   ＿＿ You have used diuretics or laxatives.
   ＿＿ You have engaged in binging and vomiting.
   ＿＿ You have usually regained lost weight.
   ＿＿ You have regained more than the lost
        weight.
   ＿＿ You consciously dress to mask your weight.
   ＿＿ You usually skip breakfast.
   ＿＿ You overeat when you are under stress,
        sad, lonely, or bored.
   ＿＿ You think about food a lot, especially
        when dieting.
   ＿＿ Once you start eating, you have trouble
        stopping.
   ＿＿ If you eat more than you think you should,
        you feel guilty.

5. Discuss the ways in which you think you would
   benefit by being slim:＿＿＿＿＿＿＿＿＿＿
   ＿＿＿＿＿＿＿＿＿＿＿＿＿＿＿＿＿＿＿＿＿
   ＿＿＿＿＿＿＿＿＿＿＿＿＿＿＿＿＿＿＿＿＿
   ＿＿＿＿＿＿＿＿＿＿＿＿＿＿＿＿＿＿＿＿＿

PART 2
(Answer These Questions *After* You Read the Book.)

(Use a separate sheet of paper if you want to expand on any of your answers.)

DATE: _____

1. Which of the following revelations from the book provided an important breakthrough in your understanding of your body, your weight, and your eating patterns? Check the ones that apply.

____ The ways that cultural norms create false dieting patterns and sabotage weight control.

____ Genetic characteristics that are unique to individuals.

____ The reasons why excess water loss leads to water retention.

____ How eating too little leads to weight gain.

____ The fact that dieters are biologically predisposed to binge when they eat.

____ The realization that dieting patterns have had a severe negative influence on the quality of your life.

____ The methods given for calculating your ideal weight.

____ The discovery of where you fit within the three diet types.

____ The guidelines outlined in your personal program for weight control.

____ The Personal Awareness Exercises.

_____ Other (please elaborate):

_____

_____

_____

2. Describe the most important way that the book has changed your approach to weight management:

_____

_____

_____

3. Describe in your own words the primary factors that you believe have led to your classification as a Starver, Skipper, or Stuffer.

_____

_____

_____

4. Record the following information:
   - Current weight _____
   - Height _____
   - Waist/Hip Ratio _____
   - Conditions compatible with low metabolic rate (list):

     _____

     _____

     _____

   - Conditions compatible with high metabolic rate (list):

     _____

     _____

     _____

   - Medical conditions compatible with obesity (list):

     _____

     _____

     _____

   - Recommended weight range listed on age-adjusted scale: _____

PART 3
Participation in Study Group

If you are willing to participate in a research project on the experiences of people using this plan, please sign the form below. You will receive instructions for tracking your progress and evaluating your results.

I agree to participate in a controlled study of my experience with the Callaway Diet. I understand that all the data I supply will be used only for purposes of research. My agreement to participate is made without any expectation of specific future benefits, such as monetary compensation or guaranteed improvement of health and weight conditions.

SIGNATURE:_____

DATE:_____

PART 4
Setting Up a Support Group

As part of my work, I am interested in evaluating the effect of group support on the success of this program. If you are willing to set up a support group (of friends, family, neighbors, etc.) with no fewer than four people, sign the form below.

_____

I agree to set up a support group with no fewer than four people who will participate in the Callaway Diet and report on their experience. I understand that all information we supply will be strictly confidential. My agreement is made without any expectation of specific future benefits, such as monetary compensation or guaranteed improvement of health and weight conditions.

SIGNATURE:_____

DATE:_____

RETURN THESE FORMS TO:

C. Wayne Callaway, M.D.
2112 F Street N.W.
Suite 703
Washington, D.C. 20037

Introduction

It was the kind of scene that made my day. Julie, a young nurse of 27, bounced into my office looking absolutely radiant.* As I examined her, she chatted about the way her career was taking off and how energetic and happy she felt. I couldn't help remembering the day I had first met Julie several months earlier. She had dragged herself into my office, listless, tired, and feeling fat and bloated. She carried 140 pounds on her tiny 5-foot-2-inch frame, and from her puffy face I could see that some of the extra weight was caused by water retention.

Her story was one I had heard many times before. "I've been dieting religiously," she complained, "and I take an aerobics class every day. I can't lose weight no matter what I do. I feel lousy and I look like a wreck. What's wrong with me—do I have some kind of hormonal problem?"

I questioned her about her diet, which was a very low 800-calorie regimen that a friend had raved about. "It sounded good, and I was doing okay at first," she said. "I was losing almost a half a pound every day. Altogether, I lost about ten pounds in three weeks. Then I stopped losing, which didn't bother me, because the diet said there would be a plateau at about that point, which would last a couple of days. I kept on the diet and I didn't cheat, but I didn't lose any more weight for a week, and then I just gave up and started using another diet, which was twelve hundred calories a day. It was a disaster! I actually *gained* three pounds in the

---

*To protect the privacy of my patients, I have changed names and personal details.

first week. Dr. Callaway, I'm a nurse, and I know it doesn't make any sense that I should have to eat *less* than eight hundred calories to lose weight. There must be something else going on."

Had Julie told that story to most people, she would have received one of several reactions:

"You must not be following the diet correctly. Are you sure you're not cheating?" Or:

"You may be one of those people who has a hormonal problem that prevents you from losing weight." Or:

"There's a great diet theory that says if you're allergic to certain foods, you can't lose weight. Why don't you give it a try?"

And so on.

There are always plenty of excuses for why low-calorie diets don't work. No one ever considers that the diet itself may be the culprit.

In successfully treating Julie's weight problem, I used the method outlined in this book, a method that has worked for thousands of patients I've treated at the Mayo Clinic, George Washington University Medical Center in Washington, D.C., and now in my private practice. It's an approach that works, even with chronic dieters—those people who *never* seem to lose weight no matter what weight-loss system is tried. But I'll tell you right up front that my approach is very different from all of the weight-loss diets you may have tried in the past.

I first became interested in the study of obesity and related conditions twenty years ago, while a resident in internal medicine at the Mayo Clinic. I noticed that at least two-thirds of the medical conditions people suffered were in some way related to nutrition, and many of them were directly related to obesity. I also saw that people were suffering psychologically as well as physically in their struggle to lose weight.

In my years on the staff at Mayo, I developed first-hand an appreciation of the pain people experience, both by being overweight and by failing in their diet attempts. It became apparent that obesity was not an easy condition to understand; rather, it was incredibly complex.

Ultimately, it became the focus of my research and clinical work to integrate a wide variety of disciplines into studying the causes and treatments of obesity—including anthropology, psychology, sociology, and the behavioral sciences. In the past twenty years I have worked with more than ten thousand people whose medical problems have a dietary basis. And I have had the good fortune to participate in work that reflects the current edge of research regarding genetic factors in body size, the behavioral aspects of weight control, the consequences of different patterns of fat distribution, and the causes and cures of eating disorders. My work has been focused in two primary areas: Identifying the different types of obesity, and researching the biological changes that occur when people go on very low-calorie diets.

This work led to the program I now use in my practice, and one which I am training others in the medical and nutritional communities to use in their treatment of eating disorders and obesity-related conditions.

This book is the first serious effort to convey this approach to a mass audience, although I have presented it on many occasions to professional groups of dieticians, nutritionists, doctors, and others. It has been a long time coming, but today the successes of this work are frequent enough that I am confident about presenting this unconventional diet approach in a popular form so that you, your physician, and your nutritionist can begin to apply the encouraging results of the research to your own permanent success.

I am often asked to appear on television news programs to comment on breaking issues related to diet and nutrition, or to be interviewed for documentaries. It was as a result of one of these experiences that I knew I had to write this book.

In early 1988, I appeared on an ABC network program called *The Health Show*. The topic was dieting, and I was on the air for only ninety seconds. In that brief clip, I described the symptoms of chronic dieting and what causes the syndrome known as "yo-yo" dieting. The network supplied my name and address at the end of the broadcast.

In the coming weeks, the letters began to pour in from all over the country. They were scribbled on postcards, the backs of grocery lists, and torn pieces of notebook paper. Many were sent to a wrong address or no address—just "Yo-Yo Diet, Washington DC"—but somehow they reached me. In over three thousand letters, case after case of dieting failure was related. These people were begging for help; they were finally ready to try to diet the right way. There was a desperate tone to many of the letters:

> I wear a size 14 and I know this might not seem too extreme, but it affects my whole life. I diet all the time to lose 10 pounds. . . . I don't want to be overweight forever.
>
> K.C. — 34-year-old woman

> I've been on every conceivable diet and my weight fluctuates up to 20 pounds at any given time. I've always dreamed of being thin, but I'm beginning to think it's pretty hopeless.
>
> B.N. — 49-year-old woman

Frequently, the letters described the many painful physical and mental symptoms that I've found to be the result of chronic dieting:

> I cannot eat more than one small meal a day without gaining weight. I'm cold all the time and my

hair and skin are dry. I feel as though my body has just stopped working.

> P.Y. — 40-year-old woman

In the past I didn't have trouble losing, but now I seem to put on weight if I eat anything at all. I'm miserable . . . and scared of what's happening to me.

> G.H. — 36-year-old man

In America today, there are millions of frustrated dieters, just like these people, who have followed all the rules but still haven't succeeded. I have written this book to help break the cycle of failure that chronic dieters experience. It is my intention to replace quick weight-loss diets that *don't* work with a scientifically valid program that *does* work. It is my sincere hope that, in the very near future, we will look back on semistarvation diets the way we currently view such archaic practices as bleeding and purging. When George Washington's physicians practiced therapeutic bleeding on him (and most likely hastened his death), they were doing what was accepted practice at that time. Today's "diet doctors," with their various formulas, diets, pills, and other gimmicks, are in a similar position. Some are well-meaning but inadequately informed. Often they are operating from an ideological rather than a scientific base. I believe that the abandonment of these false approaches will do wonders for our collective self-esteem. Once we break the pattern of dieting failure, we will then be freed to pursue the meaningful task of living our lives to the fullest.

The Callaway
Diet

ONE

The Diet Ripoff

My patients have succeeded on nearly every diet they've tried. They are the "success stories" of the nation's most popular weight-loss plans. They have lost 75 pounds with Optifast. They dropped 6 or 7 pounds in the first week by following the Fit for Life Diet. They have been remetabolized, rotated, desensitized, brainwashed, and "cured" of food addiction.

And now they are my patients. Every day I sit in my office and listen to them repeat stories I've heard so many times that I could tell *them* what they've experienced before they begin to tell me. They come to see me because they've heard me speak on television or read an interview I gave to a magazine or newspaper, but I can tell they are skeptical. They fear that my office may be just one more stop on a long journey that they fully expect to travel for the rest of their lives.

It's hard not to get angry. During the past twenty years, my colleagues and I have been involved in serious research and clinical studies designed to gain insight into the causes and cures of human obesity. We are not the multimillionaires who operate chains of weight-loss clinics that promise quick cures. We don't run big companies that sell everything from liquid protein milkshakes to amphetamine-like drugs to supplements designed to "melt off fat." You don't usually see our names and faces plastered all over the media, or

1

hear us expounding on miracle treatments on national talk shows.

It's not that our work doesn't get noticed; I have been quoted in hundreds of magazine articles and interviewed for numerous television and radio programs. In recent years there has been some real excitement generated about my work and the work of others like Kelly Brownell, a psychologist at the University of Pennsylvania who has studied the long-term effects of low-calorie diets. But even though we now have conclusive evidence, based on credible scientific research, that particular approaches can be successful in helping yo-yo dieters (who lose and regain weight frequently) finally lose weight and keep it off, our message too often gets drowned out by the roar of a $33 billion weight-loss industry that stays alive through misinformation and gimmickry.

The media must share the blame for regularly treating diet gimmicks as though they were news stories. The nation's publishers must share the blame for seeking big sales at the expense of accuracy. And even our medical and scientific communities must share some of the blame for failing to communicate our knowledge in practical and convincing ways.

The success of *Fit for Life* is a good example of the way I believe the diet industry regenerates itself from year to year, to the detriment of the public. *Fit for Life* was a multimillion-copy best seller, published by Warner Books in 1987. It was the year's *big diet,* supported by aggressive promotion and sales machinery. The Diamonds, whose nutrition degrees come from nonaccredited schools, propose in their book that it does not so much matter what you eat, but when you eat it, and in what combination foods are consumed. Their plan includes recommendations such as not eating anything but fruit before noon, and never eating protein at the same meal where carbohydrates are consumed. This is a theory that the Diamonds seem to have literally invented out of (excuse the pun) thin air, and they have offered little but anecdotal evidence to support their claims. In fact, the Diamonds's recommendations set a standard for poor nutrition; many doctors and nutritionists panned the approach when the book was published. As one said, "I couldn't possibly support a plan that tells you that food *rots* in the body."

When the Diamonds were in the midst of the media blitz that hyped their multimillion-copy best seller, I faced them in a television debate. They seemed to view me as one of the most despicable creatures known to man: a medical expert. Look at all the obese people in America, they said. Doesn't that tell you not to trust the experts? Their great claim to fame was that they were not experts, and therefore, allegedly, not "corrupted" by the Establishment. My comment that the dietary practices promoted by this book were commonly seen in people with eating disorders was shrugged off as "sour grapes." Millions of desperate dieters bought the Diamonds's line—and their book.

But where are the Diamonds now, scarcely three years later? How many of your friends are marveling about the way *Fit for Life* has given them great results? Marilyn and Harvey Diamond's year in the sun is over; their followers have long since regained the lost pounds and turned their attention to another diet.

As I write this, the rage is Optifast, the "medically supervised" liquid formula diet that has taken the country by storm ever since Oprah Winfrey modeled her svelte size 10 body for a television audience of millions. I am fairly certain that eventually Oprah will regain her lost weight, or, at least, struggle every day to avoid doing so. I don't say this cynically and I am not placing the blame on Oprah's inability to control her eating. If Oprah regains the weight, it won't be because she's weak or addicted or born to be fat or any of the other things people who fight for weight control tell themselves. In fact, Oprah is like most of the patients I see in my practice—smart, strong, motivated, and personable. And like them, she blames her past failures on a flaw in herself that won't allow her to eat normally. The day she modeled her "new body," she admitted to the press that she would have to fight every day of her life to control her hunger and keep from putting the weight back on. It strikes me that this is no way to live.

You may wonder why it is possible for people to get away with writing books that present unproven theories or dangerous practices. Freedom of speech prevents regulation of written material, giving publishers free rein to put any theory on the market, whether it is feasible or not. The only recourse the public has is the courts—and a diet has to have produced traceable harm before a case can even be made. Robert Kowalski's phenomenal best seller, *The 8-Week Cholesterol Cure,* was criticized by some medical experts from the beginning for recommending that people take three grams of niacin a day, a very high dose that can potentially lead to a variety of dangerous side effects. But the book remains on the best-seller list.

Every new miracle diet promises that it is different from all the others. But most diets are simply repackaged versions of old approaches. New and revolutionary theories don't just spring up overnight, but because we are impatient, we don't want to believe this. And so we try each new gimmick and fail once again. Current statistics show that more than one-half of adult women and one-fourth of adult men in our country go on diets two or more times every year. And the failure rate for these diets is estimated to be somewhere between 70 and 90 percent.

The time has come to call a halt to this nonsense. Surely we could find better use for the $33 billion we spend each year chasing these false promises.

Endless Stories of Diets That Failed

Proponents of the diets would like you to believe that these failures are the exception rather than the rule—people who are victims of indulgence or poor discipline or bad genes. But it's simply not so. These people are the rule rather than the exception. If you consider your own experience and the experiences of your friends and family, you will know that what I am saying is true. But *why* is it true? Later in the book, I will describe in detail what scientists have learned about low-calorie diets and why they *can't help you lose weight permanently*. I will also tell you what will work. But first, let's examine some of the *big weight-loss promises* you've been given in the past, and why these promises were not fulfilled in your experience.

1. *Diets for food addicts.* Many chronic dieters find some comfort in the thought that they are "addicted" to food. It seems to help explain why they can't stay on a diet. There are many programs that address this "addiction," most notably Overeaters Anonymous, which uses many of the same techniques as Alcoholics Anonymous. While many dieters benefit from the psychological and group-support aspects of these programs, there are some inherent problems associated with them.

First, there is no such thing as a "foodaholic," at least not in the same way as people become addicted to alcohol or drugs. Later, I will demonstrate that it is most likely the *act of dieting itself* that leads to the compulsion to eat. And often it is not a psychological trigger that sends dieters back to the refrigerator, but a series of *biological* triggers. Ignorance of the biological causes of eating behaviors makes programs like OA the wrong models for success. These programs lead to a predictable obsession with eating, a cycle of starving and binging, and ultimate failure. The goal of any feasible weight-control program should be to establish autonomy, not to create a new class of people who believe something is wrong with them.

By the time a dieter joins a program like Overeaters Anonymous, he or she is truly desperate, having tried many diets and never having achieved success. By naming the problem the dieter's *addiction* rather than pointing the finger at *unsound diets*, OA simply reinforces the idea that dieters should take the blame for not losing weight on programs that simply don't work.

There are other addiction-based theories that seem impressive because they address seemingly real biological factors. *The Carbohydrate Craver's Diet,* by Judith Wurtman, Ph.D., promotes a theory that some people have an uncontrollable craving for certain foods, caused by brain chemistry. Her second book, *Managing Your Mind and Mood Through Food*, takes the theory a step further. Wurtman's theories are not without some basis, but she has jumped the gun on research, drawing conclusions about human eating patterns based on a few rat studies. Those who follow her diet advice may be impressed by what seems a logical connection between certain foods and the way they catalyze the interaction of body chemicals. And they'll definitely delight in the frequent allowances of sweets and snacks. But I believe Wurtman has drawn many simplistic conclusions from incredibly complex data. This seems to be a case of someone taking a little bit of scientific information and carrying it too far. It is also a way of using desperate dieters as guinea pigs for unproved theories.

Stuart Berger has also made a name for himself in the mass media by relating obesity to food allergies. His *Immune Power Diet* has been frequently panned by medical experts and nutritionists. Dr. Berger says that if you eat foods to which you are allergic, they will intensify cravings, leading you to eat more. Only by eliminating offending (Berger calls them "sinister") foods from your diet are you able to begin eating normally. Although Dr. Berger proclaims that a minimum of one out of three people have food allergies, most allergists say the number is more like *1 to 2 percent* of the adult population. Further, there is no evidence that any kind of vitamin therapy can control obesity.

When I was director of the Mayo Clinic's Nutrition and Lipid Clinics during the early 1980s, I found that the assumption that people are overweight because they overeat was not borne out. National survey data shows the same thing. As many as two-thirds of the people with weight problems are not overeating. In fact, many of them eat *less* than other people of the same size. My patients at Mayo were often chronic dieters or they regularly skipped meals. As I will show in chapter 4, it is these behaviors, *not* food addictions or allergies, that lead to weight problems.

2. *Diets that eliminate food.* These are the "last chance" diets that say, in effect, "If all else fails, just stop eating." Optifast, Medifast, Herbalife, and the Cambridge Diet have all depended on formula diets. Another variation on the approach is Nutri-System, which sells low-calorie prepackaged meals. Today, liquid diets are more than a $100 million a year industry.

I mentioned earlier that I have concerns about the Optifast and other liquid protein diet programs. I have reason for these concerns—a number of my patients are victims of the liquid diet method. Perhaps a closely supervised formula program can be useful as a short-term method for the dangerously obese—say, for those who are 50 percent or more above their recommended weight. There is also a small sub-group whose poorly controlled hypertension, diabetes, or high blood fats may be brought under short-term control with such an approach. In fact, it was Optifast's original intention to serve as a solution for people with serious obesity-related medical conditions, but the program has now taken on a life of its own.

The Optifast program is sold through hospitals and

physicians, which lends it credibility as a medically supported program. A brief training session is conducted for those who will be monitoring the program—painfully inadequate for handling the complex problem of obesity.

The value of Optifast must be examined in relation to the lucrative financial incentives that exist for hospitals and consulting physicians who buy into the program. There is quite a bit of money to be made by offering the program—dieters pay about $100 a week for the liquid formula and the behavior modification classes. And, as it has gained in popularity, it has evolved from a program designed only for the dangerously obese. Current requirements stipulate that a patient must be only 15 percent above his or her recommended weight to qualify for the program. That means that a woman whose "ideal" weight is 130 pounds need only weigh 150 pounds to qualify. That's hardly what one would term dangerously obese! And radical methods such as this one should be used only when the health value of fast weight loss outweighs the benefits of a more balanced program.

Recently Optifast has added behavior modification classes designed to help dieters control their eating once they return to normal foods. In my opinion, a behavior modification approach that is not concurrent with the normal environment is comparable to locking up an arsonist and then praising him because he no longer sets fires. In fact, my post-Optifast patients usually admitted that as long as they were on the liquid formula, they weren't afraid of overeating, but once real food was made available, they didn't know how to handle it. Most gained back some or all of the weight they had lost, and sometimes even more. At the other extreme, I've seen patients who became so afraid that eating would make them lose control that they became anorexic or bulimic.

3. *Diets based on metabolic mumbo-jumbo.* These are the fad diet programs that sell like hotcakes in bookstores and become the rage (for the short time they last) because they're "different." Usually they're written by self-proclaimed diet experts with little or no credibility in nutrition, medicine, or metabolic studies. Often they're based on a research sampling of one subject—the author. Many of these diets present eating patterns that are consistent with what we see when people have eating disorders such as anorexia nervosa. An example is Judy Mazel's *Beverly Hills Diet*. It is not uncommon for diet books to be written by people who have engaged in lifetime battles with anorexia, bulimia, or other conditions. Elizabeth Taylor wrote a diet best seller last year, but today she is back to fighting the pounds that have piled back on in the interim.

Diet gimmicks rarely work over the long term, but they almost always work in the short term. That is because they are based on a very quick weight loss in the initial two or three weeks. But this so-called miracle weight loss *always* consists of two-thirds or more water. As I will discuss in chapter 4, water is lost in the early days of very low-calorie diets, but it is then retained as the diet progresses. Unfortunately, most dieters don't make a connection between the fact that they lost 5 pounds in the first week of a diet with the fact that they gained it back in the third or fourth week. But both occurrences are part of the same biological cycle.

This phenomenon has been around through Dr. Atkins, Dr. Stillman, the Scarsdale Diet, the Fit for Life Diet, the Rotation Diet, the Rice Diet, and numerous others. Sometimes these diets do worse than simply mislead people who want to lose weight—they call for methods that can make people sick. Dr. Atkins was not exactly promoting an enlightened view when he suggested that dieters consume large amounts of protein (and therefore fat), and restrict their carbohydrate consumption. On the other hand, protein deficiency was a serious problem of Judy Moscowitz's version of the Rice Diet. It is ironic that in a society where food is readily available, there are people who are suffering from nutritional deficiencies that are associated with severe conditions of famine.

A final word. Weight Watchers has traditionally earned high praise from nutritionists and medical experts. The Weight Watchers program has promoted a well-rounded, group-supported, gradual weight-loss approach. But even Weight Watchers bowed to pressure to follow the quick weight-loss route. Several years ago, it introduced the 900-calorie "Quick Start" program, possibly because it was having a hard time competing economically with programs that offered faster initial weight loss. In my opinion, Weight Watchers has compromised its credibility as a sound, effective, long-term weight-loss program by doing this. I would like to see the Quick Start program eliminated, and Weight Watchers return to a sounder approach.

Good News for Yo-Yo Dieters

Most of my patients have tried some or all of these diet programs before reaching my office. And chances are, this is not the first time you've purchased a book on weight loss. If you've already invested a great deal of time and money in trying to lose weight and keep it off, you're well acquainted with all of the programs I discussed above—plus many others.

But there is good news. As we head into the final decade of the twentieth century, the weight-control picture looks very different from the way it did even ten years ago. Those of us who have been involved in pursuing answers to the problems of an overweight society have reached a turning point in our understanding of the factors that regulate body shape and body weight. It is no longer necessary to rely on arbitrary standards, guesswork, or trial and error. During the past twenty years, while our society has been pursuing its diet gimmickry, many scientists have been doing serious research with animals and humans to gather evidence about the biological factors that lead to weight gain and thwart long-term weight loss. Based on this research, we can now begin to address some of the most persistent dieting dilemmas, including:

- Why dieters so often gain back to their prior weight and sometimes gain even *more* than they lost.
- Why it is so hard to control the tendency to binge.
- Why some people are able to eat "normally" while others get trapped in patterns of starving or over-eating.
- Why it becomes increasingly difficult to lose weight with each successive diet.
- Why some people get "stuck" and can't lose even when they eat very few calories.

Because we have learned so much about body metabolism, dietary patterns, and heredity, it is possible to treat weight problems with reliable methods. We can establish a successful weight-loss regimen that helps you determine appropriate goals, achieve those goals, and get off the weight loss/regain cycle.

If you have dieted many times, the program I outline in this book will allow you to break the yo-yo pattern of losing weight and gaining it back—or gaining back more than you first lost. If you have never dieted before but want to lose now, this program will allow you to do so without falling victim to the dieting patterns that undermine long-term weight loss. With this approach, you will feel better (both physically and emotionally), look better, be healthier, and often eat more than you do now.

False Assumptions
Have Thwarted Past Success

Our cultural biases about weight have provided fertile ground for a number of false assumptions that set us up for defeat and desperation. No wonder dieters so often fail! The popular mythology about weight and weight loss is negative and demeaning. The most damaging attitudes include:

- All overweight people are alike.
- Overweight people are gluttons.
- Overweight people are lazy.
- Overweight people lack willpower.
- Overweight people are out of control.
- Weight loss is simply a matter of eating less.
- The faster you lose, the better.
- Quick weight-loss programs should work for everyone.
- If you don't succeed, it's your fault.
- Rebound weight gain has nothing to do with *how* or *how fast* you lost the weight.
- Binging is caused by a psychological disorder.
- People are overweight because of psychological problems.

These false assumptions not only undermine your efforts to maintain weight loss, they also open the floodgates for numerous commercial programs that feed the panic: low-calorie diets, prepackaged foods, formula diets, amphetamines, hormone injections, hypnosis, jaw wiring, stomach balloons, and countless other exploitive gimmicks. Nearly all of these programs are founded on the notion that losing weight is simply a matter of eating less, and the less you eat, the faster you'll lose. And most of the time, the premise works *in the beginning*. When you starve, you lose weight. But, as I pointed out earlier, most of the weight loss is just water. For people who are not morbidly obese, it's simply not possible to lose 4 or 5 pounds of *fat* in a week. Since the scale doesn't distinguish between fat and water, many dieters are deceived into believing they've lost fat. They also don't understand that their bodies, having depleted their water stores, will begin to retain water. So, the thrill of saying, "I lost five pounds in the first week," is brief indeed.

When you go on a diet that offers quick weight loss in the first week or two, you rave about its miraculous powers. But several weeks later, when you are retaining water, regaining weight, and feeling miserable, whom do you blame? Not the diet! The great mythology is that the *diet* works; it is *you* who have failed.

If you, like most dieters, have believed these false assumptions, it's likely that you don't feel too good about yourself. If a friend lost 20 pounds on a diet and you didn't, you feel that you lack discipline. If you lost weight but then gained it back, you worry that you are unable to control your urge to eat.

The promoters of quick weight-loss diets have convinced you with their endless "success" stories that a desirable thin body is just around the corner if you follow their regimens. You buy the message and you pay the price time and again—financially, physically, and emotionally.

When you personalize the messages behind the false assumptions I've outlined above, your self-story becomes:

- "I'm a glutton."
- "I'm lazy."
- "I'm out of control."
- "I lack willpower."
- "If I didn't eat so much I would lose weight."
- "It's my fault that I can't lose weight when I go on a diet."
- "I must have a psychological problem that makes me this way."

It is impossible for any human being who believes such stories to have positive self-esteem! The reinforce-

ment of negative opinions about yourself only feeds
your discouragement—and leads to continued failure.

What is needed is a new approach to weight loss that
doesn't blame the victim for past failures, doesn't ex-
ploit the desperation of dieters with hit-and-run approaches, and *does* offer a treatment based on the current
well-researched and documented knowledge we have
about diet and weight control.

For example, contrary to popular belief, no single
diet is going to be effective for everyone. Our research
has shown that weight problems differ from person to
person, and in order to work for the long term, a
program *must* begin with a complete personal inventory. This is the crucial step that is normally missing in
diet books, and even in programs like Weight Watchers, which puts every dieter on the same number of
calories (regardless of height and weight) and the same
regimen. In this book, you will find a method for evaluating your personal weight goals and choosing one of
three plans that addresses your situation. Specifically,
this plan includes:

1. A simple, easy-to-follow explanation of what happens to your body when you diet, why low-calorie diets
lead to edema (water weight gain), binging, and a metabolic slowdown that halts weight loss even when you eat
very little.

2. A personal inventory that reveals important factors
about your genetic profile, developmental history, and
eating and exercise patterns that will form a reliable
basis for choosing the plan that best suits your needs.

3. A comprehensive plan that effectively combines diet,
exercise, behavior modification, and psychological support to help you reach your ideal weight without starving, binging, or obsessing about food.

4. A guide for evaluating your success, not only in
terms of weight loss but in terms of the quality of your

life. As you lose weight and learn more effective eating patterns, you will also develop more rewarding goals. I have found in my practice that weight problems are intricately linked with a whole series of concerns people have about achieving their life ideals.

This is not the easiest program you have ever tried—especially if you're impatient to see overnight weight loss. But if you're willing to follow my guidelines, this should be the *last* program you'll ever have to follow. It may take longer than you're used to, but consider the benefits: along the way, you'll feel great, instead of being tired, cranky, and hungry. (Many of my patients report that the return of their energy ends up being more valuable than the weight loss.) You'll learn to eat normally and healthfully and will no longer feel deprived, guilty, or obsessed with food. When you lose weight, you'll know it's really permanent fat loss, not easy-off (and easy-on) water loss.

Once you are freed from the crazy dieter's cycle that has consumed your attention and damaged your ego, you will have the time and energy to focus on all of the wonderful things that you've been putting on hold as you waited to be thin. And that's the biggest benefit of all.

TWO

The Thin Distortion

My practice is in Washington, D.C., which is like a "company town," only in this case the company is the federal government. Being the center of the political world makes Washington a fiercely competitive society town; you can fall in and out of favor in the blink of an eye, depending upon which parties you're invited to, which charity functions you're asked to chair, and whether your name is on the list for an "intimate" reception for five hundred at the White House to honor a visiting dignitary.

Living under such scrutiny can be very stressful, as the many men and women who find their way to my office tell me. And in recent years it has seemed to get worse, since "packaging" has become the road to success and power in the political arena.

Leslie's husband was a prominent government official, but before she married him Leslie had had no experience with government or with Washington society. Her mother-in-law took the new bride under her wing and supervised her society education. Leslie's job as a political wife, she was told, was to "be pretty and have children." Pretty she was—but at 5 feet 6 inches and 125 pounds, Leslie wasn't the pencil-thin ideal that she or her husband's family desired. She began a rigorous course of diet and exercise with a goal of losing 15 pounds.

Leslie was referred to me after she had been married for two years. She wanted to start a family, but she had not had a normal menstrual period for several months. At the time of her first visit, Leslie weighed only 108 pounds. She told me she ran six to eight miles every day, worked out in a gym three times a week, and kept her eating in check by skipping breakfast and eating very little lunch. She also admitted that she occasionally took laxatives and diuretics.

When Leslie stopped having menstrual periods, she was very frightened that something was seriously wrong with her. Something was: she was starving herself.

"What you're experiencing is common," I said. "It's part of a whole series of biological changes that your body undergoes when it isn't getting enough food. In a way, it's perfectly logical. Since women in famine situations are unable to nurture their babies, nature steps in and makes it impossible for them to get pregnant. That's what has happened with you. You're eating too little and exercising too much and your body thinks it's in a famine."

I explained that she would have to stop exercising completely for a while and start eating about 1,500 calories a day, divided into three meals, until her bodily functions returned to normal. And, I added, if in the future she needed to lose weight, she would have to do so in a slow, balanced way or she'd end up right back in the same boat.

Leslie looked at me with despair. "If I do that, I'll gain weight," she said. "I just *can't* gain weight."

I felt sad for this young woman, who experienced such a tremendous pressure to be thin that she was willing to sacrifice her health and even her ability to have children for the sake of 5 or 10 pounds.

If you are really interested in conquering your weight problem, it is important to understand the cultural sea in which you swim. For most Americans, that "sea" is a society that equates leanness with the most coveted rewards of human life: beauty, love, success, security, and happiness.

In our society, being fat—or even a little plump—is considered highly undesirable. The obsession about weight is so deep that many people will go to extreme lengths to be thin.

Recently I saw a cartoon that seemed to capture the extent of the obsession. Two women were standing in a cemetery, looking down at a grave. One of them was saying, "Poor Mabel . . . and she was only within five pounds of reaching her weight goal."

In her book, *The Obsession*, Kim Chernin relates this story:

> . . . a friend fell ill. She was taken with severe abdominal cramps. They grew so painful that she was unable to sleep. My friend was taken to the hospital. There, when the most severe cramps were over and the hospital staff was able to do routine physical tests, a scale was brought into the room. My friend, who had been unable to eat for several days, felt distinctly happy to see the scale. "I jumped off the bed," she told me. "I ran over to it. 'What's it say? What's it say?' I kept asking the attendants. And, when they told me, I repeated triumphantly: 'I've lost four and half pounds.' "
>
> When she was discharged from the hospital with the condition undiagnosed but possibly abdominal cancer, my friend came home. The first thing she did was to rush into the bathroom and go over to the scale.
>
> "I'd like to tell you," she said to me, "that I'd willingly gain back the five pounds rather than go through that horrible pain again. But I honestly don't know whether it's true."

Sadly, the desperation to be thin is passed on to our children—especially young girls—and the whole destructive cycle begins again. Two studies recently reported by investigators at the University of California, San Francisco, and the University of Michigan reveal that dieting to lose weight is common for girls as young as 9 years old. In the University of California study, researchers found that:

- 81 percent of the 10-year-old girls were dissatisfied with their weight and were already dieting.
- 31 percent of the 9-year-old girls worried that they were too fat or would become too fat.
- 38 percent of 11-year-olds significantly misjudged their weight.
- Only 6 percent of all girls surveyed reported being satisfied with their weight.

Researchers at the University of Michigan found that:

- More than 40 percent of 14-year-old girls believed they were overweight or "very overweight."
- 40 percent of 14- and 15-year-old girls were on diets.
- Nearly 20 percent of 10- and 11-year-old girls, and 25 percent of 13- and 14-year-old girls, were encouraged by their mothers to diet.

Girls begin to hear the thin-body hype at a very early age. Television, movies, and magazines are undoubtedly a strong influence, and many of the girls in these studies reported that their mothers often dieted to lose weight; some mothers also encouraged their daughters to diet even when they were very young. It is sad to watch these children climb aboard a treadmill that they're likely to remain on for the rest of their lives. And it is particularly disturbing when we consider the widespread occurrence of anorexia nervosa and bulimia, life-threatening conditions that occur with the greatest frequency in women between the ages of 15 and 30.

Recently I attended a buffet dinner at the home of friends, and the hostess had prepared an elaborate dessert spread on a big table. At one point I was standing next to the table talking with the hostess, when suddenly her eyes darted away from me. "Don't eat that," she said sharply.

I turned and saw her 18-year-old daughter, who was about to take a bite of strawberry cake. She grimaced and put down the cake.

"She has to lose six pounds by next Saturday," her mother explained, "so she can get into the dress she's wearing to the freshman dance."

My friend's daughter is a delightful, smart, and absolutely lovely girl, who isn't the least bit overweight. I mentioned this to her mother, who shrugged and said, "Oh, she could stand to lose a few pounds. Who couldn't? Besides, there's the dress."

"Why not save yourselves a lot of agony and just buy a different dress?" I laughed, and the daughter piped in, "That's what *I've* been saying."

It is common for mothers to project their own obsession with weight onto their daughters. Later, my friend's daughter told me that she thought about her weight all the time. "All the girls in my dorm ever talk about is dieting," she said. "It's the main topic of conversation, and every time there's a new diet, we try it."

There are many reasons why people in our society have such an intense desire to be thin. Often the desire is not a matter of frivolous vanity. Health concerns are certainly one valid reason. But overweight people are also discriminated against, both professionally and socially. For example, studies have demonstrated that overweight women have only one-third the success of thin women in interviews for colleges and first jobs. People are denied jobs or even fired because they are overweight—even when physical performance is not a job issue. Since overweight people are believed to be less competent than their slimmer counterparts, they feel the squeeze in terms of salary, too. A recent study reported in *Industry Week* magazine shows that, in today's job market, each excess pound of weight costs an executive one thousand dollars a year in salary.

Not long ago, I was contacted by the concerned family of a young military officer who had been advised three months earlier that he would be discharged if he did not lose 30 pounds in six months and meet the required weight standard. He had been dieting intensely, using laxatives and diuretics, and making very little progress. Now he faced an almost certain discharge, unless I could intervene. I contacted the young officer's superiors and told them that, although he did need to lose weight, it would be impossible for him to do so under the conditions they had stipulated. Furthermore, I told them, he had developed health complications as a result of his use of laxatives and diuretics, and these would have to be treated before I could put him on a weight-loss regimen. His superiors resisted at first ("rules are rules"), and it was only after much effort that the officer was allowed to follow a more reasonable approach.

What struck me about this incident was the arbitrary nature of the military's required weight standard; until I got involved, no one suggested that a starvation diet that included heavy use of laxatives and diuretics might put the young man at more of a health risk than being 30 pounds overweight.

Weight often becomes a point of contention in personal relationships as well. I once treated a woman whose husband made her sign a contract that she would lose 25 pounds before he would put the down payment on their dream house. This kind of blackmail is not uncommon. It effectively reinforces the belief that you have to be thin to get what you want in life.

Chasing a Fickle Ideal

During the past twenty years, our cultural ideals have become harder and harder to achieve. Studies of three groups of "ideal" women—fashion models, *Playboy* centerfolds, and Miss America contestants—bear that out. These groups were 8 percent below average weight twenty-five years ago; five years ago, the models dropped to 18 percent below average weight. Since these women symbolize physical ideals, the pressure is great for other women to follow their lead—even though the cultural standards are largely arbitrary. When we consider that 30 million American women (35 percent of the adult female population) wear dress sizes of 16 or over, it isn't hard to conclude that something is not right.

And it's not only the size 16s who are suffering. Dieters who *do* manage, through extreme deprivation, to starve themselves into too-thin bodies are able to take little pleasure in their "success." In chapter 4, I will explain why semistarvation diets lead to alterations in metabolism that are responsible for several conditions, including lack of energy, insomnia, constipation, and water retention. I once treated a Miss America contestant who was 5 feet 9 inches and weighed 117 pounds. At her natural weight of around 130, she would still have been slender, but the competitive arena of the beauty pageant had driven her to be even thinner. To achieve this, she dieted and exercised strenuously. She was finally referred to me by her gynecologist because she had stopped menstruating. He was concerned that she might have a pituitary tumor. By trying to force her weight below what was normal for her, she suffered many negative consequences. Simply put, her body was rebelling.

Although women in our society are frequently judged against the abnormally thin "ideal" represented by models and beauty pageant contestants, this bias toward leanness is rare on a global scale. International studies on body preferences show that in 90 percent of societies, both men and women prefer women with "female" body shapes—that is, with broader hips and thighs. In these societies, women of higher socioeconomic status tend to weigh more than women of lower status. Plumpness carries prestige.

But in the United States and other affluent societies this pattern is often reversed. Here, the higher the education and economic levels, the lower the body weight and the more likely it is that women will be dieting. In societies where food is readily available and manual labor isn't essential, thinness becomes equated with self-discipline rather than economic hardship.

Even our own society hasn't *always* been focused on a thin ideal. In the late nineteenth century, being plump was considered healthy and a sign of affluence. Doctors and other authorities were actually writing books with titles such as *How to Be Plump*. Insurance companies actually charged heavier people less because they believed they were less likely to contract tuberculosis and other infectious diseases. And don't forget that Lillian Russell, the great turn-of-the-century femme fatale, weighed 210 pounds.

I once treated a very pretty young actress who was eager to lose 20 pounds but was having trouble staying on a diet. She was upset when she came to see me because she felt it was urgent that she lose the weight quickly. "My agent says I'll never get on television unless I'm thinner," she told me.

"I can help you if you're willing to go about it the right way," I replied. "But if you aren't a successful actress, it isn't because you're a few pounds overweight. Maybe it's because you have a lousy agent."

People are always putting their lives on hold until they lose those few pounds, but sometimes people's lives get put on hold forever because they never lose the weight. I recently got a phone call from a friend who was trying to decide whether to accept a job in another city. She was depressed because she had gained a few pounds and her clothes didn't fit right. She couldn't make up her mind what to do. "Maybe I'll move when I lose the weight," she said. Even though my friend was very talented in her field, she could not visualize herself as successful without also visualizing herself as thin. Extra weight—whether it's 10 pounds or 50— often becomes a limiting factor in people's lives. I told my friend, "If Franklin Roosevelt could be president of the United States in a wheelchair, you can start a new job even though you're ten pounds overweight."

Cultural-Biological Dissonance

There's nothing wrong with cultural norms, as long as they serve a purpose. But when our cultural ideals are not consistent with the biological realities, it becomes a tug-of-war. I call this inconsistency Cultural-Biological Dissonance (CBD). With CBD, it's easy to predict what will happen: If the cultural standard for body shape is too low, people will undereat to try to become thin. If the cultural norm is plumpness, they will engage in deliberate overeating to gain weight (thus the books on how to be plump).

It has been my experience that, in the case of weight ideals, CBD leads to a number of occurrences:

1. People will starve (or stuff) themselves in an attempt to meet the ideal.
2. Biological adaptations will resist drastic changes in body weight, leading to a pattern of frequent failure to achieve cultural ideals.
3. This failure will be attributed to culturally accepted notions such as lack of willpower and self-control, and the victim will be blamed.
4. This progression will provide fertile ground for the emergence of exploitive industries that promise weight loss (or weight gain) with special diets, pills, or other gimmicks.

Usually, by the time people have reached a clinical setting, they are quite discouraged and even feel guilty about their presumed weakness. But when we begin to explore the various ways that CBD affects our community and personal standards, and leads to unsuccessful dieting behavior, these people often experience an immediate feeling of relief. There's a definite shift in attitude—even a catharsis—that occurs when they really see how the deck has been stacked against them. Only then, when they understand the cultural pulls and the biological realities, can they finally do what is necessary to lose weight.

One of my patients, Marissa, was a good example of Cultural-Biological Dissonance. Marissa would have been considered the "ideal" by most people. A ballet dancer with a leading international company, she was 5 feet 3 inches and weighed 107 pounds. Nevertheless, under pressure from the artistic director, she would go off to spas repeatedly and semistarve to bring her weight down even lower. When Marissa returned from her spa trips, she regained the weight very quickly because of severe water retention.

Eventually, Marissa reached a state where she sometimes gained as much as 15 pounds of water in a week! At that point, of course, she was unable to perform because of extreme bloating. The harder she tried to lose the weight, the worse things became.

At last, with proper information about how to eat, Marissa was able to reverse this pattern. But her intense pursuit of a culturally determined but biologically unrealistic weight goal had nearly ruined a very promising career. Today she is well and no longer retains water, but she's one of the lucky ones. Many other dancers in her company have gone on to develop anorexia nervosa and bulimia, eating disorders that are now commonplace among dancers, models, and actresses.

Rethink Your Goal

I believe that we shortchange ourselves when we try to impose uniform standards of beauty. It's comparable to making an aesthetic choice between a painting by Monet and a symphony by Stravinsky. We place value in the diversity of artistic expression, but we cannot see that human diversity has value.

It may seem odd to read a "diet book" that spends so much time questioning the value of being thin. I assure you, it is not because I am in favor of people being fat—my entire career has been devoted to helping people achieve normal, healthy weights. But I have seen people wreck their health for the sake of losing 10 or 20 pounds, and that's crazy. I have seen people being duped out of thousands of dollars to pursue treatments that don't work. And I have reached the conclusion that the only way to begin a successful weight-loss program is to put it in its proper perspective, along with your other goals.

It is likely that you haven't discovered the secret to successful weight control. You may have tried dozens of diets, sought help from doctors, psychiatrists, hypnotists, personal trainers, and gurus—all to no avail. Perhaps your focus has been so completely trained on the "ideal" that you have been unable to see the obvious solution: a plan of action that is personalized to fit *you*, not a passing cultural fad.

THREE

Different Sizes, Different Shapes

When you picture yourself at your perfect weight, what do you see? Most of the people I've treated had some idea of what would be perfect, even if they had never experienced it. As one woman said to me, "I'll know it when I get there."

If you've been trying all your life to mold your body into a thin ideal, you may have trouble accepting that certain genetic factors affect your shape and weight. Yet, if we were talking about your height, you would have little trouble seeing the connection between you and your ancestors. I have rarely had a patient say, "Help me be three inches taller." But you've been conditioned to think of your shape as a different matter. Height is viewed as being inherited, biological, and not your fault. Weight is viewed as acquired, behavioral, and even moral.

The first step in resolving your weight problem is to understand your body. You are the product of your genetic heritage, your personal history, and your environment. The way this is commonly described is that your body is the product of both "nature" and "nurture." "Nature" refers to the givens about your shape and size that were determined before you were born— genetic factors that result in the resemblance you bear to members of your family. "Nurture" refers to the environmental factors such as eating and activity patterns that have influenced your growth. As much as 50 percent of the variation in size and shape from one person to another appears to be a result of genetics and the influences of your early environment. The remaining 50 percent is a result of eating patterns, physical condition, and ongoing environmental factors.

It's important to view your body as the particular result of genetics, history, and behavior. Your biological profile will become the foundation for determining how much you should weigh and how best to get there.

Few diet books deal with this issue. They discuss weight loss and dieting as if they were simply matters of learning to eat less, or, worse, primarily psychological or even moral issues. By ignoring biological factors, they can better convince you that their "generic" diets will work for anybody. It is certainly easier to sell a magic formula than it is to formulate a serious program based on the complex design of human physiology.

But I urge you to pay careful attention to the biological factors we will discuss. Only when you understand and acknowledge the givens of your biology can you be released from the trap that has prevented you from reaching and maintaining appropriate goals.

Set Point or Set Range?

Genetics plays an important role in your body size—and an even greater one in your body shape. Each of us has what might be called a "genetically programmed natural weight range." Very simply, this is the percentage of your weight variation that is controlled by genetic factors. The extent of this range varies from person to person, because you don't exactly inherit your size and shape in the same way as you inherit eye color and blood type; there is no single "fat gene" or "thin gene" that gets passed on. Your shape is usually the result of multiple genes that you inherit from your parents and grandparents. Every time people reproduce there is a genetic shuffle. This is why fraternal twins (who come from different eggs) are only half as likely to be of similar shape and size as identical twins (who come from the same egg), in spite of having the same parents and growing up in the same household.

Dr. Albert Stunkard of the University of Pennsylvania conducted groundbreaking research in this area with his two studies of adoptees, conducted in Denmark and Iowa. Stunkard and his colleagues studied the adult heights and weights of people who were adopted as children and compared them with the heights and weights of both their biologic and adoptive parents. Both studies confirmed that adoptees have weights and heights more similar to their biologic parents than to their adoptive parents.

The "Twin Studies" conducted by Dr. Claude Bouchard and his colleagues at the University of Laval, in Quebec, Canada, demonstrated that our responses to over- and undereating may also be affected by genetics. In Bouchard's study, twelve sets of identical twins were fed an extra 1,000 calories daily for 3 months. When the results were evaluated, it was found that, within each pair, the twins had gained about the same amount of weight. However, there were wide differences among the sets of twins. For example, one set gained less than 5 pounds, while another gained 20 pounds. In a second test, food intake was held steady and the twins increased energy expenditure by several hours of exercise each day. Again, within each pair, the responses were similar, but the results varied widely among the sets of twins.

These studies demonstrate a clear genetic factor in our body size and shape. They also suggest that when you try to deviate too far from your "set range," your body simply resists.

I have found this to be true in my research and clinical work. People's attempts to reduce to a body size that doesn't correspond to their genetic propensity have been no more successful than those of people who once stretched themselves out on racks, thinking they could grow taller.

Bob was such a case. A bright, successful lawyer of 48, he had been fighting a weight problem during his entire adult life. When he came to see me he weighed 250 pounds. It was the highest his weight had ever been. At various times in his life, Bob had dieted down as far as 160 pounds, which would be considered low for his 6-foot-1-inch height and stocky build. He was never able to maintain this low weight, and when he started regaining, he usually gained back more than he had lost.

I asked Bob to list the members of his family who had builds similar to his. He named his maternal grandfather and his mother's brother as being most like him. His mother and sister, he told me, tended to be a little on the heavy side, but they were shorter and had smaller frames.

As he was growing up, Bob was always bigger than his classmates, but never obese. He played football in high school and maintained a weight of about 190 through college.

"In law school, I wasn't getting much exercise and I felt flabby, so I went on a diet and lost about twenty-five pounds," he said. "It wasn't that hard to lose it, but it was pretty hard to keep it off because my schedule was so crazy. From then on, it was one diet after another."

Let's look at how Bob's dieting actually created a weight problem that he would not otherwise have had. As a boy, Bob was big, but he wasn't fat. Some people are simply genetically bigger than others. His size was not related to eating problems; in fact, when he played football in high school, Bob was in excellent shape.

His first problem came when he stopped being so active. He still didn't have a problem with eating, but he was no longer burning as many calories as he had in high school, so he gained weight. At that point, what Bob should have done was begin a program of regular exercise. Instead, he chose a quick weight-loss diet. As we will discuss in the next chapter, diets that are very low in calories have a number of effects: they encourage a pattern of weight loss/weight gain; they create a predisposition to binging; and, when they are repeated a number of times, they encourage a rebound weight gain that is usually more than was lost in the first place. Once Bob started the semistarvation diet cycle, he set up the circumstances that led him to have a long-term weight problem. Bob always would have been bigger than average, even if he had not started dieting. But he would not have been fat, and his adult weight would have been stable at about 190 to 200 pounds. The extra 50 pounds Bob had gained was the result of dieting, not genetics.

How Your Body Gets Its Shape

Several mechanisms may account for these genetic differences. One theory, supported by recently published research, suggests that genetic factors might be involved in the way our bodies metabolize food.

The studies in question indicated that some babies are born with metabolic rates that burn calories as much as 10 percent slower than the norm, and are therefore more likely than others to get fat in later life. Metabolism is a complicated operation. In essence, it is the sum of all the biochemical processes; the metabolic *rate* refers to the rate at which you burn calories. Some of the babies studied were able to burn calories much faster, which means they were able to consume more food without gaining weight. Those with the slower metabolic rates were likely to gain weight faster.

In one study, reported by researchers in the *New*

England Journal of Medicine (S.B. Roberts, et al., 1988), it was found that energy expenditure at 3 days of age was more than 20 percent lower in some infants. These infants showed greater weight gain at 3 months than those with higher metabolic rates. This led to the hypothesis, as yet unvalidated, that some people are born with a propensity for gaining weight. The popular press picked up the implications of this possibility with a vengeance in 1988. But very little is known for certain and quite a bit more research will be conducted before firm conclusions are reached.

Other studies still in research point to the possibility that certain individuals are born with a tendency to produce fat cells more frequently—a condition that leads to weight-control problems. The amount of fat in your body depends on how many fat cells you have and how much fat is in each cell. The more fat cells you have, the more fat you are able to store. As the cells get bigger, it becomes harder to pack more fat into them, so new cells are created—even in adulthood—to store excess fat.

Once fat cells have been produced, they never go away, even if you reduce your weight. When you lose body fat, the fat cells grow smaller, but that doesn't mean it's easier to stay thin. In fact, the smaller the fat cells, the more avidly they store fat and the more reluctant they are to give it up. If you have more fat cells than average, it will be more difficult for you to achieve average weight—even if the cells are a normal size.

It is important to note that, in itself, the tendency to have more fat cells is not a health problem. Most of the complications of obesity are associated with how large the fat cells are, not with their number—something we'll discuss in more detail later.

Measurements of fat cell numbers and sizes are still research tools, not available for clinical evaluation. However, some of the exercises we will do later in the book will help you determine whether you have more than the average number of fat cells, larger fat cells, or both. As one general guideline, it appears that the earlier in life your initial weight gain occurred, the more fat cells you're likely to have.

It is wrong to surmise from this data that certain people are "doomed" to be fat. The fact that a person has a particular predisposition or tendency does not imply that he or she is trapped in a weight that might be unhealthy. However, research on the genetic tendencies of people to be fatter or leaner contradicts the notion that "all fat people are alike." To the contrary, individual biologies differ from one another; each person has a unique genetic status that must be considered in order for weight management to be successful.

"Apple" and "Pears"— Bad Fat vs. Good

Not all body fat is equally bad from a health standpoint, and for this reason, not every weight problem is the same. We can begin by separating the cosmetic implications of fat from its health implications. People who carry extra fat within their abdomens ("apple" shaped) suffer a number of health risks, while people who carry extra fat in their hips and buttocks ("pear" shaped) seem not to suffer any health risks as a result of extra fat. This is a fundamental distinction because health implications will be important in determining how much weight you should lose, how you should lose, and how fast you should lose.

It is commonly believed that any excess weight is unhealthy, but it is primarily excess abdominal fat that presents health risks. Every obesity-related medical problem has so far been related to "belly" fat. For example, men with the greatest waist/buttocks ratio (those with pot bellies and no buns) have up to four times the normal risk of heart attacks and twice the risk of diabetes. On the other hand, excess hip, buttock, and thigh fat, when it is not accompanied by excess fat in the abdomen, has never yet been associated with known health risks. (In chapter 5, I will give you a formula for calculating a "safe" percentage.)

The tendency toward excess belly fat is more common in men, since the male hormone testosterone favors belly fat, while the female hormone estrogen favors hip and thigh fat. Some men (and a few women) may have "normal" weight-for-height ratios when compared to standard weight tables but may still be "metabolically obese"—meaning that they are at greater risk for weight-induced diabetes and heart attacks because they have too much abdominal fat.

The distinction has to do with the way fat-cell activity differs in the abdomen and the thighs. All fat cells have receptors for norepinephrine, the adrenalinelike chemical that is used by your autonomic nervous system to regulate stores of fat. In the thigh cells, alpha receptors predominate, which favor the storage of fat. But in the abdomen there are more beta receptors, and these favor the release of fat. This released fat (known as free fatty acids) circulates in the blood, and when it reaches the liver, it can interfere with the metabolism of insulin, the hormone needed for the normal metabolism of fats, sugars, and proteins. This can bring out adult-onset diabetes. It can also increase the liver's production of triglycerides and cholesterol, conditions that lead to heart disease and strokes. As belly-fat cells grow larger, they become more resistant to insulin, forcing your pancreas to make more. If it can't make enough, your blood sugar level rises, heightening your potential for developing diabetes or heart disease.

In contrast, fat in the hips and thighs seems not to present health risks. In fact, thigh-fat stores may actually serve an important biological function for women. During puberty and early pregnancy, fat is easily stored in a woman's thigh-fat cells. In late pregnancy and during breast feeding it is easily mobilized and made available to nourish the fetus and, later, to provide the fat content of breast milk. The fact that most women try to attack the fat on their hips and thighs is a good example of Cultural-Biological Dissonance. When food was scarce (which was the case through most of human history) women who were genetically predisposed to store fat in their thighs and hips may have been more likely to give birth to live infants and to keep them alive than women who did not have such energy stores available in their bodies. Seen in this perspective, typical female fat distribution patterns—that is, fat in the hips and thighs—have been partially responsible for the survival of the human race!

Remember, too, that most societies value plumpness and generous hips and thighs in women; in these societies, cultural values are consistent with biological survival. In our society—especially during the past two decades—famine has not been an issue and the cultural distortion of abnormal leanness has predominated.

Given this background, we can appreciate why the distribution of fat in your body may be more important than how much you weigh. And we can begin to see the limitations of weight-loss programs that focus solely on how many pounds you lose, rather than on more important questions: How much do you need to lose? Where do you need to lose it? How can you lose it? And how can you best evaluate your success, using criteria related to the quality of your life—not just the number on the scale.

Any sound weight-control program *must* consider the distribution of fat as a critical factor. Programs with the simplistically stated goal of just weight loss, be it 20 or 30 or 40 pounds, fall short, because you can lose weight and be thinner but still have a dangerous level of belly fat. For this reason, I have developed a new way to determine your healthy weight that takes into account the consequences of where your fat is located.

It is important that you not be frightened by your genetic inheritance or see genetic traits as the stumbling block to your weight loss. To the contrary, once you understand your personal biology, your potential for success increases because you are less likely to pursue weight-loss gimmicks that don't take the factors of heredity, personal history, and environment into consideration.

FOUR

Famine or Feast

Most of my patients are "experts" on the subject of weight loss. This is not surprising, since many of them have devoted their lives to losing weight. Their information has been culled from hundreds of magazine articles, dozens of books, a variety of clinics and programs, and, of course, from endless discussions with friends and family members about how to lose weight. A woman once told me that she had rarely been in a group where the subject of dieting didn't come up.

This vast store of knowledge includes many so-called facts that everyone knows—such as, the less you eat, the more you lose. Or drinking eight glasses of water a day will help you lose weight. Or you gain 1 pound for every additional 3,500 calories you eat. Many of these so-called diet facts are the very things that have been sabotaging your success.

In spite of the huge investment people make in learning how to lose weight, the success rate is dismal. It is almost unprecedented for humans to invest so much energy for so little reward, and yet that's exactly what has happened in our society. Although fad diets are regularly abandoned, there has been no mass stampede against the diet gurus whose methods have repeatedly failed; to the contrary, the weight-loss industry has never been more profitable. When diets fail, dieters meekly stand in line to take the blame.

The tendency for self-blame is understandable in light of the common belief that overweight people are lazier, less in control of themselves, and more gluttonous than people of normal weight. As a result, dieters feel self-disgust when they see the hard-lost pounds rolling back on.

But, as we've already pointed out, cultural hype does not change biological reality, and the truth is that most diet failures have nothing to do with inadequacies on the part of dieters. The problem is the misconception people have that starving is the appropriate method. Most people would agree that the quickest way to lose weight is to stop eating. And it's certainly true that if you starve, you're eventually going to get thinner. But in the meantime, your body puts up a good fight to save you from the effects of starvation. Consider these facts:

When you go on a diet and lose several pounds very quickly, most of that loss is water, not fat. And it is very soon followed by water *retention*, as your body adapts to preserve its stores of sodium, potassium, and other essential nutrients. When sodium is retained, so is water.

Starving leads to a slowing down of your metabolic rate, another protective mechanism your body uses to prolong survival. With a lowered metabolic rate, you burn calories more slowly and lose less weight—even on very low-calorie diets. Low metabolic rate also leads to intolerance of cold temperatures, fatigue, sleep disturbances, dry skin and hair, light-headedness when standing, memory impairment, and ultimately depression.

Starving predisposes you to binge once you start eating again. This binging is controlled by biological signals; it is not simply a lack of discipline or loss of self-control.

The evidence is clear: when you abide by the popular notions of how to lose weight, chances are you'll end up gaining. And the discouragement caused by failure, combined with the biological depression caused by a lowered metabolic rate, will only reinforce your despair and further undermine your self-esteem.

Marketing studies conducted for a major weight-loss organization found that, when dieting, most women expect to lose between 2 and 3 pounds a week and most men between 3 and 5 pounds a week, or they'll discontinue the program by the third week. To remain financially successful, commercial operations try to meet this expectation, even when they know that most of the early weight loss is from water and that a water retention cycle will eventually follow. Virtually all the experts— from the Surgeon General to well-respected popular health and nutrition writers such as Jane Brody to the researchers and clinicians I cite in this book—agree that diets designed to meet these expectations always fail over the long term.

Recent animal and human studies have led to greater understanding about what happens to your body when you diet. In this chapter I will describe the latest findings about the factors that have been preventing your long-term success: water loss and water retention, lowered metabolic rate, and the connection between low-calorie diets and binging.

The $33 Billion Gimmick: Water Out and Water In

Most popular diets are very low in calories. (Be aware that even when a diet presents a "different" method, it usually boils down to being very low in calories. For example, *Fit for Life* doesn't talk about counting calories, but if you follow the regimen, you will probably find that you are on a low-calorie diet.) Depending on your size and dieting history, you may be able to lose large amounts of weight very quickly when you go on these programs. I've seen people drop more than 15 pounds the first week, and 5 to 10 pounds the second week, on semistarvation regimens of fewer than 1,000 calories. But more than two-thirds of this loss is water.

There is a simple explanation for why you lose so much water on a low-calorie diet, and why most very low-calorie diets are also low in carbohydrates. Your brain and red blood cells need blood sugar (or glucose) to function. Blood sugar comes from carbohydrates. If your body is not getting enough glucose to supply the brain and red blood cells, your liver will break down its stored sugar (glycogen) and send it into your bloodstream. When the glycogen stores are depleted the liver will begin to convert the amino acids from your body's muscle protein into sugar. The glycogen and proteins in the liver and muscles are tree-shaped, branched molecules surrounded by water. There is three times as much water present as there is protein and glycogen, so every time the liver breaks down an ounce of glycogen or protein, three ounces of water are released from the cell, transported to the kidneys, and excreted as urine. This is why you lose so much water in the initial stages of a low-calorie diet. It's the basis for the initial rapid weight losses with the popular "protein sparing" and "ketogenic" programs that eliminate or severely restrict carbohydrates.

A study conducted by Doctors Mei-Uih Yang and Theodore Van Itallie at St. Luke's-Roosevelt Hospital at Columbia University in New York demonstrated the effects of low-carbohydrate diets. Two groups of people each ate 800 calories a day, one with carbohydrates and one without. The group on the low-carbohydrate diet lost almost twice as much weight as the one on the high-carbohydrate diet, but *water loss accounted for all of the difference*. Each group had the same fat loss.

Rapid water loss is the $33 billion diet gimmick. It looks good on your bathroom scale and it raises your hopes. But the initial water-weight loss is completely meaningless in terms of your ultimate goal. You are not losing fat; you are not getting leaner. It's only a trick, a gimmick, the temporary side effect of not eating enough carbohydrates to supply your brain and red blood cells with their essential fuel, which is blood sugar. That's *all* it is. If you lose 3 to 5 pounds (or more) in the first week of a diet, you can count on the fact that what you've lost is mainly water.

Not only does rapid water loss produce no benefits, it actually causes harm. Along with water, you lose essential nutrients, such as sodium, potassium, magnesium, calcium, and phosphorus. Sometimes this leads to dehydration and dizziness when standing up quickly. Drinking extra water doesn't help because it is simply excreted by the kidneys—it doesn't replace the water that was lost from *within* the body's cells. Taking salt tablets causes the kidneys to retain some water and may prevent some of the dizziness, but it doesn't replace water within the cells, either. And it won't help to take calcium, potassium, or magnesium supplements because, unless the glycogen and protein are remade within the cells, the supplements simply pass out of the body in the urine.

Proponents of rapid weight-loss programs argue that this early "success" is a great motivator for people to stay on their diets; if progress is slow, they'll get discouraged. I know this seems to make sense, and I agree that motivation is crucial to a successful diet. The problem is, the faster you lose water, the more likely you are to develop subsequent problems with water retention. Your body won't tolerate having its protein and glycogen stores broken down and its stores of water depleted for long without trying to compensate. Your kidneys adapt and begin to retain sodium; with sodium, they also retain water. This is one of the causes of the plateaus you experience with prolonged dieting.

Furthermore, when you go off your low-calorie diet

and begin eating more food, you immediately regain water weight. This is called "refeeding edema." I have seen people gain 5, 10, or even 15 pounds within 24 to 48 hours of going off a very low-calorie diet. This weight gain is all attributable to fluid retention. We are not entirely sure what causes refeeding edema; my speculation is that, in part, the increased amount of insulin released to metabolize your food promotes refeeding edema, since insulin has been shown to foster sodium and fluid retention by the kidneys. New evidence indicates that there is also a hormonal signal, yet to be identified, that causes fluid retention. There is no question, though, that it does occur, and understandably, it creates absolute panic in dieters.

It becomes a vicious cycle. If you were eating 800 calories a day on your diet, and then you started eating more—say 1,200 a day—you probably gained weight from water, even if you were actually burning more than 1,200 calories a day. This no doubt led you to conclude that you gain weight on 1,200 calories and must eat much less to lose weight. You can see how this thinking leads to an endless cycle of weight loss/weight gain.

At the George Washington University Medical Center, I once treated a 29-year-old woman who had been on and off diets since she was a teenager. When she came to the clinic, Kathleen, who was 5 feet 4 inches and weighed 165 pounds, had been involved with a well-known commercial program for about three months, and she had been eating fewer than 1,000 calories each day. She was now experiencing massive edema—one of the worst cases I'd seen. She had been on the commercial program for about one month when she started gaining weight. The nurse at the center where she weighed in every day told her that the weight was due to water retention and suggested she take vinegar tablets as a diuretic! She did, but it only made the problem worse. During the week of Christmas, she gained 9 pounds, even though she was rigidly sticking with her diet.

Naturally, by this time Kathleen was getting discouraged. In January she went off her diet. Within four days of normal eating, she had gained *15 pounds*. That's when she came to the clinic.

Kathleen's problem was so severe that it took six months on an adequate diet for her to lose the water weight she had gained as a result of extreme dieting and diuretic use. She was also losing a slow and steady ½ pound of fat per week. At six months, she weighed 144 and showed no further signs of edema. Her weight loss continued at a rate of 1 to 2 pounds per month, and within another five months she stabilized at 125 pounds, the lowest her weight had ever been.

Kathleen's case is an extreme example of the fluid-retention problem that dieters experience, but all diets that promote quick weight loss—which is primarily water—lead to some form of fluid retention.

Refeeding edema is the most common cause of fluid retention among American women. Yet, this subject has received scant attention in our medical textbooks. The problem is widespread and is well recognized in countries where malnutrition is pervasive—most of us have seen pictures of children with bloated bellies caused by severe malnutrition. However, in the United States, water retention and the resulting puffiness is usually blamed on premenstrual changes or on unknown causes. It is frequently treated with diuretics, which only makes the problem worse. Diuretics cause an initial water loss, but this is quickly compensated for with water retention.

Your Furnace Gets Turned Down

A review of the effects of starvation on humans—specifically, victims of famine, concentration camp survivors, and political activists on hunger strikes—shows similarities to people who undertake self-imposed low-calorie diets. It now appears that starvation or semistarvation (defined as consuming fewer calories than your body burns at rest) leads to adaptive changes in the metabolic rate that slow down the rate of weight loss and also produce a number of side effects, including tiredness, dry skin and hair, intolerance to cold temperatures, constipation, and depression.

Your metabolic rate, as we pointed out in chapter 3, refers to the rate at which you burn calories. This is measured by first determining your Resting Metabolic Rate (RMR), which is the number of calories you would burn in 24 hours if you did not eat or perform any activity. This is done by measuring how much oxygen you burn and how much carbon dioxide you produce first thing in the morning before you've eaten and while you're lying quietly. A normal day's activity will add at least 30 percent to the RMR; manual labor or aerobic exercise will add even more.

Here's an example: A person with an RMR of 1,500 calories, and who has an average level of activity, burns about 1,950 calories per day. This is the number of calories that person can take in without gaining fat. Some athletes will burn twice or even three times their RMRs because of vigorous and prolonged exercise. If they don't eat enough to compensate for their energy expenditure, they will develop some of the problems that are commonly seen in chronic dieters. I've seen dancers, gymnasts, and distance runners who were eating 1,500 to 1,800 calories a day, but burning nearly 3,000 calories. If their metabolic rates had not slowed down to adapt to this imbalance, they might have starved, even though they appeared to be consuming a "normal" amount of food.

Some of the variation in RMR is related to your eating patterns. In a study I conducted with Cecelia Pemberton, the former chief dietician at the Mayo Clinic, we found that meal-skipping led to a lower RMR. We compared RMRs and eating patterns in more than two hundred patients in our Nutrition Clinic. Those who skipped breakfast and lunch began the day with the lowest RMR; those who skipped only breakfast were a little higher; those who had a small breakfast (less than 10 percent of their total calories for the day) did a little better; three-meal-a-day eaters with larger breakfasts did even better. And the chronic overeaters, who had six or more feedings per day, had metabolic rates above normal.

Eating increases the metabolic rate even more, partly because energy is required to digest and absorb food and partly because eating food leads to the release of insulin, which increases the production of two heat-generating hormones, tri-iodothyronine (T-3) and nor-epinephrine (NE).

Thus, from a dieter's standpoint, the three-meal-a-day eater has two advantages over the meal-skipper. He or she *begins* the day burning calories at a higher rate. And following each meal, more calories are burned. In our Mayo Clinic study, we estimated that an average 40-year-old woman, 5 feet 5 inches tall and weighing 150 pounds, would burn between 100 and 200 calories more each day if she ate three equal meals rather than one large meal in the evening. This doesn't sound like much until you consider that a 100-calorie-per-day difference between what you eat and what you burn would result in a 10-pound weight change each year; a 200-calorie difference would produce a 20-pound change. Small daily "errors" can produce large cumulative changes over the long term.

We're Programmed to Fight Starvation

Why does meal-skipping lower RMR in the first place? The answer to this question is found in human history. Often we fail to appreciate just how closely linked our biological control mechanisms are with those of our ancestors.

In our society, there is an abundance of food; however, for much of the world—and for most of human history—famine has been an ever-present threat. In the face of repeated famines, those of our ancestors who were biologically best able to adapt by burning calories more slowly were more likely to survive. Indeed, we are *by definition* the offspring of survivors. Those who couldn't adapt had little chance of living long enough to have offspring. We have inherited the survival mechanisms. Even today, when our bodies think they are being starved—that is, if we are consuming less food than we burn at rest—our RMRs are automatically lowered. To use a contemporary example, Bobby Sands and the other Irish Republican Army prisoners who fasted in protest during the late 1970s survived between seventy and eighty days; had they not been able to adapt, they would have survived only three or four weeks.

With severe or prolonged food scarcity, the RMR may fall to less than half of normal. I have seen women with anorexia nervosa whose RMRs were as low as 500 calories per day. At that level, they were not burning enough calories to keep warm even in the summer.

The decline in RMR (combined with water retention) halts your weight loss, even if you stay on a very low-calorie diet. The less you burn, the slower you lose—and the more you gain if you go "off the wagon" and overeat.

Not only can we adapt to food scarcity by lowering our metabolic rate, but it now appears that each time we starve, many of us adapt more quickly. Over aeons, humans and other animal species have developed a biological "memory." Previous exposure to starvation improves our ability to survive the next time around. This might explain why the first time you dieted, you probably lost weight, but the more often you dieted, the harder it became to lose.

This was demonstrated in animal studies conducted by Dr. Kelly Brownell and his colleagues at the University of Pennsylvania, along with Dr. M.R.C. Greenwood, then professor of biology at Vassar College.

Their experiments involved feeding one group of rats a high-fat diet so they would gain weight, while a second control group was fed standard rat food. After the first group of rats had gained weight, half of them were then switched back to the standard food and given as much to eat as the leaner rats. Researchers recorded how long it took them to return to normal weight. Once they had returned to normal weight, the researchers then returned them to the high-fat diet and measured how long it took them to get back to being as fat as the rats who were not put on the standard diet.

When they had regained the weight, the previously dieted fat rats were then placed back on the standard diet. The second time they dieted, it took them twice as long to lose the same amount of weight they lost the first time. And when they were again placed on the high-fat diet, they gained back their original "fat" weight three times faster.

If such responses can be shown in laboratory animals, there is probably a biological basis for the phenomenon. In fact, most chronic dieters experience a similar pattern. The first time they go on a low-calorie diet, they lose weight fairly easily. But the more times they lose and gain weight, the longer it takes to lose the next time they diet, and the faster they regain the same amount of weight when they go off their diets.

When you think about it in a positive light, the increasing ability to survive starvation only shows how

well our bodies are designed. Not only can we adapt to
starvation by burning fewer calories, but we actually
improve our ability to do so each time we face famine.
You may not find this particularly encouraging news,
but I believe that this new understanding can provide a
better foundation for a new approach to weight loss.

In my clinical work at the Mayo Clinic and George
Washington University Medical Center, I concentrated
on devising methods for restoring metabolic balance. It
appeared to me that a weight-loss program could not
be effectively started until the metabolic rate of the
dieter was nearly normal. If it was too low—which was
usually the case with chronic dieters—the body would
simply fight the diet and make it harder to lose weight.
Once the metabolic balance was restored, I experimented
with various calorie levels until I found those that would
promote a slow, steady weight loss without being low
enough to trigger the body's defenses against starvation. I tested these calorie levels on patients and developed a reliable set of recommendations based on these
tests. They are incorporated into the diet program that
you will be given in this book.

The Downside of Metabolic Imbalance

If your metabolic furnace is turned down, there's
more at stake than just your difficulty in losing weight.
The hormonal changes that create the slowdown also
account for a host of adverse side effects that severely
impair the quality of your life. These include fatigue,
depression, sleep disturbances, intolerance to cold, blue
fingers, dry skin and hair, constipation, lightheadedness,
and distortions in your perception of time and space.

These side effects usually catch dieters by surprise.
Most people I've treated believe that dieting is sup-
posed to create an energy boost and even euphoria.
(That's what they've been told.) They assume their symp-

toms are "all in the head," and try even harder to pull themselves together. It rarely occurs to them that their diet may be the culprit.

Why does a low metabolic rate cause these symptoms? Here's how it works:

Your metabolic rate is regulated by your thyroid hormone, thyroxine (T-4), and tri-iodothyronine (T-3), which is the form of the thyroid hormone that regulates how much heat you produce and how many calories you burn. By itself, T-4 has little effect on your metabolism. But when it is converted to T-3, it increases the metabolic rate. The signal to increase the conversion of T-4 to T-3 is the insulin produced by the pancreas. As we have already discussed, low-calorie (and especially low-carbohydrate) diets reduce the production of insulin; this reduces the conversion of T-4 to T-3 and your metabolic rate slows down.

Insulin also affects the production of norepinephrine (NE), the adrenaline-like chemical that your brain and sympathetic nervous system use to transmit messages. NE is involved in the regulation of pulse rate, blood pressure, mood, appetite, and other neurological functions.

When you eat a meal, insulin causes an increase in NE production. When you starve or skip meals, NE production slows down. As a result, chronic dieters often have slow resting pulses and low blood pressure. Sometimes this causes dizziness and even fainting. I've worked with dieters who were told that they had experienced seizures after passing out several times upon standing. But a careful analysis confirmed that they were simply victims of a drop in blood pressure caused by the reduced production of NE and impaired responsiveness of their sympathetic nervous system.

In extreme cases, chronic dieters develop a blue discoloration of their extremities, a condition known as "acrocyanosis." When this occurs, the cause is often (erroneously) ascribed to the vascular disorder Raynaud's Phenomenon, but with a correction of their low metabolic rates, hand color returns to normal.

The Binging Rebound

As if to add insult to injury, there is now evidence that starving sets up a biological predisposition to binging.

When patients confess their binging episodes to me, they're usually embarrassed. What could be better proof of their weak wills than the inability to control their stuffing? But I explain to them that there is a biological basis for this aspect of dieting, too. In fact, binging doesn't occur without a background of starving.

Emily, age 34, had always been self-conscious about her weight. When she came to see me, she weighed 140 pounds—a little heavy for her height of 5 feet 7 inches. She spoke enviously of her sister, who was two years younger and maintained a weight of 109 pounds effortlessly.

Emily had been dieting on and off since high school, usually going on very low-calorie programs. She started binging when she was in college. "I would diet most of the week, but at least twice a week I'd binge on ice cream and chocolate. I couldn't help myself," she told me. In the years since college, Emily had continued to alternate dieting and binging. And in her late twenties, she became bulimic.

Not all bingers are bulimic, but the starve-binge cycle can lead to bulimia as a last-resort effort to control weight. Bulimics induce vomiting after episodes of binging—in severe cases, they may repeat this more than 15 times a day. Some bulimics also engage in frequent use of laxatives. Bulimia is a very serious ailment. Chronic bulimics may tear the linings of the stomach and esophagus, suffer colon damage from overuse of laxatives, and, ultimately, end up with cardiovascular complications, and even death.

Emily's pattern was to eat between 1,000 and 1,200 calories a day. She skipped breakfast, ate a light lunch, and consumed most of her calories in the evening. Her binging episodes usually occurred about twice a week, at night, and consisted of eating ice cream and other sweets, mostly chocolate. "I can't just eat a normal amount," she said. "Once I start, I can eat a quart of ice cream and a bag of cookies." After these binging episodes, she forced herself to vomit.

Emily called herself a "compulsive eater." Like most dieters, she considered her low-calorie eating "good" and her binges "bad." And she didn't recognize the connection between the two.

There are many theories about the psychological factors that trigger binging—such as the tendency to seek comfort in food or to view it as a substitute for love. These theories may have validity in individual cases—and later we'll talk about some of the psychological issues related to obesity. But all the counseling in the world can't stop binging behavior when its source is the biological rebound effect of starvation. Understanding what causes binging will allow you to change the circumstances that set it up, and to deal with the confusion, fear, and frustration you experience when you feel out of control.

Nearly everyone considers binging an aberration. But binging is a *normal* consequence of starving. Lengthy research with both human and animal subjects has shown that a very low or irregular intake of food sets off an impulse to binge when food becomes available.

For example, this dynamic was seen in survivors of German concentration camps who were recovering from extended periods of starvation. It was noticed that the survivors had a tendency to overeat, some consuming as many as 5,000 calories per day. Long after they had reason to fear future food deprivation, they continued to eat more than they had before their starvation experience. Over a period of years, many became obese—a reaction with obvious psychological implications, but which I believe has a biological basis.

One of the most famous human studies of binging in humans was conducted by researchers Janet Polivy and Peter Herman, then at Northwestern University, using two groups of women students. The first group consisted of chronic dieters and the second group consisted of normal eaters.

The two groups were asked to taste ice cream. Before the tasting, they were given either one or two milkshakes or nothing. Following a milkshake, the normal eaters consumed less ice cream than they did on empty stomachs. After two milkshakes, they consumed even less. In contrast, the dieters ate *more* after consuming one milkshake and still more after two milkshakes.

Polivy and Herman explained this phenomenon by referring to the dieters as "restrained eaters"—that is, once they broke their restraint, they found it hard to maintain control. While these findings might support the theory that some people have psychologically-related problems that make it hard to control food intake, animal studies reinforce the premise that there is a biological basis to binging behavior. Groups of rats fed either sugar water or plain water, respond in the same way.

Consider also the survival pattern of wolves. In the summer, when food is readily available, the wolf eats several times during the day and rarely a large amount. But in the winter, the wolf may go two to three weeks between kills, then kill a large animal, stuff itself, and go to sleep to prolong its stores of food. If the wolf is startled, its first reaction is to vomit. The vomiting is triggered by a survival mechanism—the wolf can't run away with a full stomach.

The signals that trigger binging are the same protec-

tive mechanisms that hoard water and conserve energy.
Your body is simply trying to survive during what it
perceives as a famine.

But when you don't know that binging is reinforced
by biological signals and is therefore a normal response
to severe dieting, you can easily draw self-accusatory
conclusions about your behavior when you overeat. It's
scary to feel out of control, and this is the way you feel
when you start to binge. You look for psychological
explanations. Or you "try harder" the next day by starving even more. But the harder you try and the more
you deny yourself, the greater likelihood you have of
binging.

This was Emily's pattern. Her inability to stop binging
scared her, and she hadn't found a solution. Two years
before she came to see me, she had joined Overeaters
Anonymous to find help for her "food addiction." But
since her problems with food were strongly biological,
OA didn't help to control her binging.

Emily was started on a 1,600-calorie diet and instructed to eat three meals a day, regularly spaced, and
no snacks. This plan was designed to bring her metabolic rate, which was 20 percent below normal, back to
normal, and to make sure that she was eating enough
throughout the day to avoid setting off the starvation
defenses that would trigger binging.

During the first three weeks of the diet, Emily only
had one binging episode, and it was on a day when she
had skipped lunch. Her metabolic rate rose seven percent, and she suffered refeeding edema and gained 5
pounds of water. But this water weight would eventually come off as her metabolic rate returned to normal.
Even with the water retention, Emily told me she was
very happy. It amazed her that she didn't have the urge
to binge. Her "terrible addiction" simply did not exist.

After two months, Emily's metabolic rate was level,
she was eating three meals a day, never binging, and

losing weight at a rate of about 1 pound per week. It took her seven months to lose down to 124 pounds, which was a more realistic weight for her build, and now, four years later, she still maintains that weight. Seven months is a long time in popular dieting lore, but it's clear to see by Emily's glowing face that she thinks it was worth it to do it right.

At the Mayo Clinic, I once treated a 40-year-old woman who is an even more dramatic example than Emily. Paula, at 5 feet 8 inches tall and weighing 220 pounds, had a twenty-year history of dieting. For ten years she had been bulimic—skipping breakfast, eating a light lunch, and stuffing herself at night. During this time she was having a lot of trouble with her marriage, and often in the evenings, after she and her husband had an argument, she fled in the car. On these occasions she would stop, buy junk food, and stuff herself.

Paula's bulimia was so severe that we hospitalized her. In the hospital, we persuaded her to eat 2,000 calories, an idea she initially resisted, since her normal weight-loss diet was 1,200 calories or less. But she needed to eat more to avoid the starve-binge cycle. She remained in the hospital for six weeks, and during that time her metabolic rate went up and she stopped having the desire to binge.

But, despite what we told her, Paula connected her binging with her marital problems, and she didn't really believe there was a biological basis. She assumed that once she returned home, she would still want to eat when she had an argument with her husband.

A week after she was discharged, Paula and her husband had an argument. As before, she escaped in the car. But when she stopped and bought food, she found, to her amazement, that she didn't have the urge to eat it. She continued to drive around, but eating was no longer associated with her "flight" behavior.

Overeating Creates
Metabolic Havoc, Too

If you regularly consume far more calories than your system can metabolize comfortably, you will experience an increase in your metabolic rate as your body works harder to metabolize and store the excess food. An abnormally high metabolic rate carries a host of side effects, but they are the opposite of those seen in people with low metabolic rates. High metabolic rates are associated with intolerance to heat, heavy perspiration, rapid pulse, nervousness, and irritability.

Furthermore, obesity and the accompanying high metabolic rate places you in the danger zone for severe medical consequences, such as adult-onset diabetes, high blood pressure, high blood fats, and heart attacks. The answer here is to eat less. How much less and how to do so is outlined in chapter 8.

The Solution:
Strike a Metabolic Balance

If the biological realities I've outlined in this chapter make you feel discouraged, don't be. Mother Nature is not working against you—she's protecting you. Once you learn to listen to your body, to understand what has happened to you and why, and to accept nature's wisdom, you can begin to enjoy success.

The key is to strike a metabolic balance, which means eating enough food, but not too much, and getting regular exercise. This sounds simple—and it is—but you need to know how to evaluate your past history and current metabolic status, how to individualize your eating and exercise program, how to set the right goals, and what to expect along the way. As always, make sure you consult with your physician before beginning this or any other diet program.

If you've never (or only occasionally) dieted and have not yet experienced the side effects I've described, you may be tempted to go on one of the endlessly available low-calorie programs. If you do, you'll probably lose quickly. But consider the long-term consequences. When you start off on the path of starving, you can only expect to end up with the same problems that chronic dieters experience.

FIVE

Your Personal Inventory

Not all overweight people are alike, and no single program is suited to every need. The personal inventory is an important first step in finding the most effective diet approach for you. Is this not logical? Think of how guilty and frustrated you've been when diet programs seemed to work for others but not for you. Your body seemed to be fighting you every step of the way; you felt out of control and hopeless.

Now you can take back control. These inventories will give you a realistic way to view yourself as a dieter and help determine which approach will be most effective. There are two inventories. The first provides a means for calculating your best weight range, using new methods developed by research scientists that are more individualized than the standard Metropolitan Life Insurance Company Height and Weight Tables, revised in 1983.

The second inventory determines which diet approach will work best for you, based upon your dieting history, your eating and exercise patterns, and your current metabolic rate.

PART 1:
Find Your Right Size and Shape

Most dieters have two goals: they want to achieve a *healthy* weight and shape, and they want to achieve an *attractive* weight and shape.

We can calculate your healthiest weight range and body-fat distribution with some accuracy. But what if you are within a healthy weight range and are not satisfied with the way you look? The key to success is to avoid conflicts between your health and your cosmetic ideals. Health risks occur when your weight is too far above or below your normal range. Furthermore, as I mentioned in previous chapters, you cannot arbitrarily decide to change your basic shape anymore than you can arbitrarily decide to grow three inches taller.

Let us also lay to rest the notion that you can be "too fat" but you cannot be "too thin." In my career, I have treated many people who came dangerously close to killing themselves, and over a dozen people who have died because they tried to be too thin; the hazards of anorexia nervosa are well documented. If you're like most of the chronic dieters I've treated, your efforts to achieve an arbitrary weight standard have led to a whole series of health-related physical symptoms, which we'll discuss in detail later.

This is not to say that you're stuck with a weight and shape that you find unattractive. You have plenty of room to move within your normal range. If you have an unhealthy fat distribution, according to the guidelines I will explain, and any weight-related medical conditions, you *must* lose. And if your weight is above the healthy range I give you, it's certainly advisable that you lose. Even if you'd just like to be slimmer for cosmetic reasons, you can do that—as long as you keep your metabolic rate normal and avoid the starve-binge cycle.

Don't Believe the
Height/Weight Tables

How do you find out your best weight? The Metropolitan Life Insurance Company Height and Weight Tables are commonly regarded as a reliable standard, but they are sadly lacking for individuals. They were first developed for the company to use as a guideline for making decisions about health risks and mortality rates. They are based on the thousands of people who bought insurance policies, and they show the weights at which the fewest numbers of policy holders died—that is, the weights at which they were *statistically* most likely to live to old age.

In recent years, the tables have been the subject of much criticism. For one thing, they are derived from individuals who purchased life insurance—and these people are not necessarily representative of the entire population. But more questionable is the way the heads were counted in these studies. The analyses were actually based on the number of *policies*, not on the number of individuals. That means if a man who purchased four policies died, he was counted four times! Finally, the heights and weights themselves are in question; in some cases, they were obtained by asking the person taking out the policy, rather than by taking an independent measurement.

Even if the methods had been reliable, the tables should be applied to groups, not to individuals. They have three serious limitations in calculating the right weight for individuals:

1. They do not distinguish body fat from body weight. Although heavier people generally have more fat than lighter people, this does not hold true for everyone. For example, football players, weight lifters, and some other athletes would be considered overweight by the tables, but they have normal or less than normal body fat. At the other extreme, some people are normal by the charts, but they have excess belly fat and less body muscle, along with diabetes, high blood pressure, or other conditions associated with obesity. These people are "metabolically obese," even though their weight is "normal." They need to reduce their weight.

I recently saw a patient who was a very good example of this. Joe was a 16-year-old high school football quarterback. He came to see me after his coach threatened to throw him off the team for being above the weight standard. Joe's coach had given him six weeks to lose 15 pounds, and Joe had been dieting strenuously to reach the weight that would allow him to stay on the team. While he was dieting, two things happened: first, his performance actually *suffered* because he was starving himself and his metabolic rate had dropped to about 15 percent below normal; and second, as his metabolic rate slowed down, he also stopped losing weight.

Tests revealed that Joe had a high muscle-to-weight ratio and very little fat in his abdominal area; in other words, although he was heavier than the weight standard, Joe was actually lean.

I contacted Joe's coach and gave him this information. I also told both the coach and Joe's mother that if he got started now on a pattern of dieting extremes, he would set up a cycle that could lead to obesity and other health problems in adult life. Fortunately, they took my advice. Joe stopped dieting and his performance improved. The last time I heard from him, he told me proudly that he had made the all-star team.

2. The tables don't adjust for age. Although there is still debate, most experts agree that modest weight gains with age are probably not harmful. Indeed, the insurance studies suggest that optimal weights are at or slightly below average weights, and average weights increase as we get older.

3. The tables don't distinguish where the fat is located. As we've discussed earlier, the location of fat is related to the determination of healthy body weight. Specifically, a number of health problems have been documented as related to a high percentage of abdominal weight; if your excess weight is primarily in the hip and thigh area, it appears not to present specific health risks.

More useful than the Metropolitan Life Insurance Company Height and Weight Tables is a three-point evaluation that includes: (1) a measurement of body composition to determine how much of your total weight is fat and how much is lean; (2) a measurement of your waist-hip ratio to indicate whether your weight distribution is healthy or unhealthy; and (3) a height-weight chart that includes age as a factor in calculating ideal weight.

A truly accurate measurement of your body composition can only be done in a clinical setting. The test that is most widely available measures the impedance to a small electrical current that is sent from your ankle to your arm (or some other part of your body). Generally, the normal amount of body fat for men is 14 to 20 percent of the total body weight; for women, it is 16 to 24 percent.

However, the other two measurements can be calculated with a great degree of accuracy at home. And, unless you are an athlete or perform strenuous physical exercise, these two readings will indicate whether your fat-to-lean ratio is high. In other words, if your total weight is above the recommended level, and you are carrying more than a healthy percentage of weight in your abdominal area, there's a good chance you're carrying a high percentage of overall fat.

Your New Personalized
Weight Standard

This new formula for determining your correct weight is more useful for you as an individual than the Metropolitan Height and Weight Tables. You can reliably use it as a personal standard because the results are based on factors unique to your body rather than on group ranges.

A determination of your ideal weight range will be based on two tests:

1. A comparison of your total body weight with the recommended standard range on the new Age-Adjusted Height/Weight Table.
2. A measurement of your waist/hip ratio, which will tell you if your weight distribution is healthy.

1. Calculate Your Ideal Weight Range

A. Weigh yourself on a reliable scale and measure your height.

B. Refer to the Age-Adjusted Height/Weight Table. This table redefines standard weight ranges, taking age into account.

C. Find the numbers that apply to your age and height. This is your "normal" range.

2. Find Your Waist/Hip Ratio

Your waist/hip ratio will tell you about the distribution of fat in your abdomen versus your hips and thighs.

A. Stand straight in front of a full-length mirror. Using a tape measure, measure the distance around the smallest part of your waist. Check the

AGE-ADJUSTED
HEIGHT/WEIGHT TABLE

Gerontology Research Center
Recommended Weights in Pounds for Both Sexes

HEIGHT	(BY AGE)				
	20–29 YR	30–39 YR	40–49 YR	50–59 YR	60–69 YR
4'10"	84–111	92–119	99–127	107–135	115–142
4'11"	87–115	95–123	103–131	111–139	119–147
5'0"	90–119	98–127	106–135	114–143	123–152
5'1"	93–123	101–131	110–140	118–148	127–157
5'2"	96–127	105–136	113–144	122–153	131–163
5'3"	99–131	108–140	117–149	126–158	135–168
5'4"	102–135	112–145	121–154	130–163	140–173
5'5"	106–140	115–149	125–159	134–168	144–179
5'6"	109–144	119–154	129–164	138–174	148–184
5'7"	112–148	122–159	133–169	143–179	153–190
5'8"	116–153	126–163	137–174	147–184	158–196
5'9"	119–157	130–168	141–179	151–190	162–201
5'10"	122–162	134–173	145–184	156–195	167–207
5'11"	126–167	137–178	149–190	160–201	172–213
6'0"	129–171	141–183	153–195	165–207	177–219
6'1"	133–176	145–188	157–200	169–213	182–225
6'2"	137–181	149–194	162–206	174–219	187–232
6'3"	141–186	153–199	166–212	179–225	192–238
6'4"	144–191	157–205	171–218	184–231	197–244

Source: Adapted from Reubin Andres, Edwin L. Bierman, William R. Hazzard, eds., *Geriatric Medicine* (New York, McGraw-Hill, 1984).

mirror to be sure the tape is parallel to the floor.

B. Still standing straight in front of the mirror, measure the distance around the largest part of your buttocks. Check to be sure the tape is parallel to the floor.

C. Divide your waist measurement by your hip measurement: this is your waist/hip ratio. Healthy ratios are:

FOR WOMEN: .70 to .75, with above .80 considered dangerous.
FOR MEN: .80 to .90, with above 1.0 considered dangerous.

Example: A woman with a waist measurement of 33 inches and a hip measurement of 42 inches would have a waist/hip ratio of .78, which is higher than the safe level recommended for women. The number was achieved by dividing 33 by 42.

3. Evaluate the Results

You have a healthy weight if (1) your weight is within the appropriate range on the Age-Adjusted Height/Weight Table, and (2) your waist/hip ratio is within the safe range of .70 to .75 for women and .80 to .90 for men. Depending on your score, you should determine your weight-loss goal in one of the following ways:

A. High Weight and High Waist/Hip Ratio

If your weight is above the level recommended for your age and height and your waist/hip ratio is above the safe level for your sex, you should proceed as follows:

1. Lose weight to reach the highest number of your healthy weight range.

2. Remeasure your waist/hip ratio.
3. If your waist/hip ratio is still high, lose to the midpoint of your weight range, then remeasure. Most people who are at the midpoint of a healthy weight range have a waist/hip ratio within a safe range. If you are an exception, and your waist/ hip ratio is still high when you are at the midpoint of your healthy weight, continue to lose weight slowly, to the bottom number of your healthy weight range.
4. If your waist/hip ratio is normal when you are at the top or middle of your healthy weight range, you do not need to lose any more weight to be healthy. If you want to lose more weight for cosmetic reasons, you may do so—but do not go lower than the bottom number on your range.

Example: You are a 35-year-old woman, 5 feet 7 inches, who weighs 164 pounds and has a waist/hip ratio of .78. Your healthy weight range is between 122 and 159 pounds, with the midpoint being about 141 pounds. Your waist/hip ratio will probably be .75 or below by the time you have lost 23 pounds and weigh 141 pounds. If you continue to lose weight, you should not lose below your bottom weight of 122 pounds.

B. Healthy Weight and High Waist/Hip Ratio
If you are within a healthy weight range, but your waist/hip ratio is high, follow the directions for point A above, beginning with number 3.

C. Healthy Weight and Safe Waist/Hip Ratio
If both your weight and waist/hip ratio are within a healthy range, you do not need to lose weight for health reasons. If you decide to lose weight for

cosmetic reasons, do not go below the bottom number of your healthy weight range.

D. Weight That Is Lower Than the Healthy Range

If you are naturally thinner than normal and have no negative health symptoms, you do not need to gain weight just to be within the range on the table. It would be difficult to do so anyway, because the more you eat, the more your body will burn. Don't waste your money on high-calorie or protein supplements.

However, if your weight is lower than normal and you have dieted to get there, you may have gone too far. I see many people who are underweight but have eating disorders, such as anorexia nervosa or bulimia, that are hazardous to their health. I also see people who have dieted down to a lower than normal weight, but who suffer the symptoms associated with low metabolic rate, which we will discuss in the next section. As you will see, these symptoms both compromise your health and diminish your sense of well-being and ability to perform.

PART 2:
Find Your Dieting Profile

In part 1 of the inventory, you calculated how much you need to lose, based on the Age-Adjusted Height/Weight Table and your waist/hip ratio. Now we will define your best diet plan, based on three factors:

    1. Your dieting history
    2. Your metabolic score
    3. Your eating and activity patterns

After seeing thousands of patients at the Mayo Clinic, George Washington University Hospital, and now in my own practice, I have concluded that there are three typical dieter profiles. Contrary to popular belief, there is no such thing as a "generic" diet program that works for everyone. Your dieting history matters because, as I described in the last chapter, the number of times you've dieted has conditioned your body to be resistant to "starving." The exact extent of resistance can be gauged by finding out if your metabolic rate is very low, moderately low, or high. Finally, your typical eating and exercise patterns must be taken into consideration, because they too have influenced your weight-gain and weight-loss cycle.

In my practice, we use the latest equipment available to measure Resting Metabolic Rate (RMR). The self-administered tests I've devised for this book are admittedly subject to variations, and they can't measure any unique health circumstances. However, based on your answers in these tests, we can determine with a reasonable amount of accuracy which profile you fit. Treatments based on the symptoms and behavior patterns of these profiles have had great success in our clinical work.

A note of caution: Sometimes people whose tests show a low metabolic rate dispute the findings, arguing that they have always been "driven" or are "workaholics." But when we talk about energy, we are not referring to stress-related or Type A behavior. Real physical energy is related to the efficiency with which your body metabolizes food, not the extent of your motivation or drive.

To find your best dieting profile, first take the three tests below. Then compare your answers with the descriptions of the three dieter profiles that follow.

Your Dieting History

Check the statements that apply to your dieting history.

____ You began dieting before the age of 18.

____ You have started a new diet at least ten times in the past ten years. ✗

_✓_ You have lost weight on previous diets, but always or usually gained it back within two years. ✗

____ You have lost weight on previous diets, but always or usually gained back *more* than your original weight. ✓

____ Your past diets have been high protein/low carbohydrate, extremely low calorie, or modified fasts. ✗

____ You have trouble losing weight even when you eat very little. ✗

____ On one or more occasions, you have lost 5 pounds or more in a single week. ✗

____ On one or more occasions, you have gained 5 pounds or more in a single week. ✗

YOUR METABOLIC SCORE

Do You Have These Symptoms of Low Metabolic Rate?

Check the symptoms that you have:

____Often cold, especially hands and feet

_✓_Dry skin and hair

_✓_Constipation and water retention*

_✓_Fatigue ✗

_✓_Loss of sexual interest ✗

_✓_Lightheadedness upon standing

_✓_Pulse rate under 60** per minute

_✓_Frequent depressed feelings ✗

Do You Have These Symptoms of High Metabolic Rate?

Check the symptoms that you have:

__✓__Often warmer than others
_____Sweaty, moist skin
_____Frequent bowel movements
_____Shortness of breath with mild exertion X
__✓__Excessive snoring at night; drowsiness during the day
_____High blood pressure (more than 140/90)
_____Pulse rate over 90** per minute
_____Frequent mood swings X

*Test for Measuring Water Retention
Push your finger firmly down on your shin bone and hold for 5 seconds. Note whether there is an indentation. If you push against muscle or fat, the skin will bounce back up. If there is water between the cells, it will be displaced laterally and the dimple won't fill in immediately. The longer the indentation remains, the more water is present.

**Test for Measuring Pulse Rate
Place a clock with a second hand by your bed. When you wake up, before you get out of bed, count your pulse rate for 30 seconds. Then multiply the result times 2 to equal the number of beats per minute.

Evaluation These are symptoms that are consistent with low and high metabolic rates. If you checked four or more symptoms on either side, it is very likely that your metabolic rate is abnormally low or high. There are other conditions that can cause low or high metabolic rate (such as too little or too much thyroid hormone). If your physician excludes these conditions, then your high or low metabolic rate is probably related to diet.

YOUR EATING AND ACTIVITY PATTERNS

Check the statements that describe normal patterns
for you.

___✓___ You always or usually skip breakfast.

___✓___ You feel compelled to eat when you are under
stress, angry, bored, or excited. ✗

___✓___ You are more hungry after you begin to eat than
you were before you started. ✗

_____ You aren't sure what physical "hunger" feels like. ✗

___✓___ You usually overeat when you're alone. ✗

___✓___ You consume 60 percent or more of your daily
calories in the evening. ✗

___✓___ You snack frequently during the day.

_____ You take laxatives or diuretics after you eat.

_____ You try to eat as little as possible every day.

_____ When you overeat one day, you try not to eat
much the following day.

_____ You never feel hungry in the morning.

_____ There are certain foods that seem to give you
comfort when you eat them. ✗

_____ You have had bulimic episodes—binging followed
by vomiting.

___✓___ You do not have a structured exercise program. ✗

_____ You exercise more than an hour daily.

Scoring Your Answers

Your answers to the three sets of questions will define
your treatment method. From the standpoint of effective treatment, I have found that there are three primary dieter profiles. You may have fit each of them at
one time or another in your life; right now, based on
your symptoms and patterns, you will fit one of the
three more closely than the others.

The three profiles are:

- **TYPE 1: The Starver**
- **TYPE 2: The Skipper**
- **TYPE 3: The Stuffer**

Compare your answers to the questionnaire above with the following descriptions to find the diet program that is likely to be most effective for you.

Type 1: The Starver

The primary characteristic of the Starver is a *long-term, repeated pattern of semistarvation on low-calorie diets.* The Starver may have a history of ten, twenty, even thirty years of regular dieting.

CASE HISTORY: THE WOMAN WHO STARVED HERSELF

Marilyn, at 45 years of age, was 5 feet 6 inches tall and weighed 180 pounds. Since there was a history of obesity in Marilyn's family, she had been conscious of her weight since she was very young and had been dieting for nearly twenty-five years.

When she dieted, Marilyn chose the starvation route; her diet plans usually allowed between 800 and 1,000 calories per day—well below "starvation" level for a woman of her size.

Finally, after many years of losing and regaining weight, Marilyn arrived at the Mayo Clinic in complete frustration. The first time I examined her, Marilyn said she was eating only about 800 calories per day, explaining that she had lowered her calorie intake because she had stopped losing weight on her previous 1,000-calorie diet. But now she was finding that it was hard to lose weight even on 800 calories. Furthermore, Marilyn was frightened by the many symptoms that accompanied her diet—including extreme lack of energy, feelings of depression, dizziness, severe bloating, and puffiness.

But perhaps her greatest fear was that she was losing control of herself. She told me that she used to be a cheerful, easygoing person, but lately it was all she could do to summon enough energy to drag herself through the day, and she was distressed by the way she found herself snapping at her children or overreacting to the most insignificant incidents. She felt her marriage was crumbling, too. Her husband complained about her being so tired; every night she went to bed shortly after dinner and there was little time for her to relax with the family.

An evaluation of her RMR showed it to be 28 percent below normal. This explained Marilyn's symptoms and also her inability to lose weight, even on a near-starvation diet.

The first task was to get Marilyn's metabolic rate back to normal, to relieve her symptoms, and to make it possible for her to lose weight. This meant increasing her daily calories to 1,500—a full 700 more than she was currently eating. When I told her that she would have to begin eating more food, Marilyn was alarmed. "If I can't lose weight on eight hundred calories, I'll blow up like a balloon if I eat that much," she protested.

Marilyn's reaction was typical of the fear most of my patients feel when I tell them they have to begin eating more in order ultimately to lose weight. It goes against everything they've ever believed about dieting, and initially they are distrustful. As Marilyn said, "Are you telling me the truth when you say I can't lose unless I eat more? Or are you *really* telling me that I'm going to be fat for life and I might as well accept it?"

I carefully explained the sequence of water loss/water retention and the way her body was conditioned biologically to resist starvation. She agreed that it made sense intellectually. "I have trouble with it psychologically," she said, "because it just doesn't seem like a diet. But I have to do something—so I'll try it."

When chronic dieting has led to metabolic adaptations as severe as Marilyn's, the initial phase often involves water retention and actual weight gain. Marilyn gained 6 pounds of water in the first three weeks and she panicked. She was practically in tears when she came to see me. "You tell me it's just water and it will go away, but this voice in my head tells me that I'm eating more and that's why my scale shows the extra pounds."

"Put your scale away," I told her. "It's irrelevant right now. Tell me about your symptoms. Are they better?"

Marilyn admitted that she felt better than she had in a long time. "I didn't realize how lousy I felt until I started to feel better," she laughed. "I have so much energy now, it scares me. And another thing—I've stopped thinking about food all the time and I'm not always hungry. But it still upsets me that I've gained six pounds."

"Try to look at it this way," I said. "You haven't actually put on fat. You're just experiencing a temporary water retention, and that's really a *good* sign. It means the diet is working. After your metabolic rate returns to normal, you'll lose this water. So try to be patient, and whatever you do, don't cut down on your food."

Marilyn did stick it out, in spite of her fear. Since her metabolic rate had fallen so low, it took her two months to lose the water. After four months, she had lost 10 pounds—and these were 10 pounds of fat, not water. After a year of slow, steady weight loss, Marilyn was down to 155 pounds.

Better still, she was feeling better and eating normally for the first time in more than twenty years. She told me that the sign that really proved the program's success was when her 12-year-old son said, "Gee, Mom, it's nice to have you back!"

Marilyn's was a true success story, but often when I tell it, people react negatively—a year seems a long time to lose only 25 pounds. But is it? Is one year a long time to achieve a permanent loss of body fat (not just water) and put an end to a lifetime cycle of weight loss and weight gain? How many cumulative years do most dieters spend losing and regaining weight? It's certainly worth considering, in light of all we know about the failure rate of quick weight-loss diets.

You can evaluate whether you are a Starver by comparing your questionnaire answers to the following points of the Starver profile.

YOUR DIETING HISTORY

- You began dieting at an early age and have been dieting off and on ever since. Starvers tend to be long-term dieters; frequently, they begin starving because of the natural weight gain experienced during puberty or pregnancy. (In extreme cases, this leads to anorexia nervosa.)
- You have started a new diet at least ten times in the past ten years—probably more often. Some Starvers are *always* on a diet cycle, beginning on Monday, binging by Thursday, beginning again the following week, and so on.
- Although you have lost weight on past diets, you have always gained it back. Sometimes you have gained back more than your original weight. This rebound weight gain happens as you begin to eat normally.
- Your diet choices have tended to be low-calorie or semistarvation plans that severely limit your intake of complex carbohydrates. These induce immediate water loss, followed eventually by water retention.
- You have had the experience of losing or gaining large amounts of weight (5 pounds or more) in a single week—the result of the water loss/water retention cycle.
- Now you find that even when you eat very little you are unable to lose as much as you once did.

YOUR METABOLIC SCORE

You checked four or more of these symptoms in the test for Metabolic Score:

- You often feel cold because you're not burning enough calories to keep your body warm—even during the summer.
- Your skin and hair are dry due to inadequate levels of T-3, the active form of thyroid hormone.
- You have problems with constipation, puffy skin, and bloating, because your stomach and small intestine have slowed down and delayed emptying, and your kidneys are retaining sodium and water.
- You are fatigued and experience sleep irregularities. Your pulse rate is low—fewer than 60 beats per minute. Reduced insulin production affects the production of norepinephrine, the adrenaline-like chemical that your brain and sympathetic nervous system use to regulate pulse rate, blood pressure, sleep patterns, and energy levels.
- You are frequently depressed. There is a metabolic basis for this. Along with your other symptoms, the reduced production of norepinephrine also influences your moods. Your biologically-induced depression adds to the burden of the emotional distress you already feel as a result of your many dieting failures—and the fact that you feel out of sync with the culturally ideal body shape and size.

YOUR EATING AND ACTIVITY PATTERNS

- You often feel more hungry after you begin to eat than you were before you started. This leads to your belief that you are subject to uncontrollable cravings; in fact, it is the normal reaction to starving we discussed in chapter 4—when food becomes available or you begin eating, a biological binging drive occurs.

- You may take laxatives or diuretics after you over-eat; these lead to water loss followed by greater water retention. You might also take amphetamines or over-the-counter diet aids to block your hunger. In the extreme, you might exhibit bulimic behavior—starving, binging, and inducing vomiting after you've binged.

   Most people believe that binging is a symptom of the Stuffer profile. But it is the chronic Starver who binges, not the chronic overeater.

- In addition to frequent dieting, you may exercise heavily, even obsessively. Heavy exercise, combined with a low-caloric diet, only lowers your resting metabolic rate further.

ATTITUDES THAT
CONTRIBUTE TO YOUR PREDICAMENT

Psychologically, you are far more interested in meeting the cultural norm than are people who fit the other two profiles. Indeed, you are willing to starve yourself to that end! Your motivation to lose weight is extremely high; even repeated failures have not persuaded you to stop, because you haven't understood what is happening. Not only do you deprive yourself of physical nourishment, you also deprive yourself of emotional nourishment and self-pride. You *always* assume that a failed diet is *your* fault . . . not the diet's.

✳ Type 2: The Skipper

The Skipper may have some of the same symptoms as the Starver, although not as many and not as severe. Your metabolic rate is slightly lower than normal (about 5–10 percent below average). But the primary characteristic of the Skipper is *a pattern of eating two-thirds or more of your daily calories in the evening.* When you consistently eat in this pattern, your body stops receiving hunger signals at appropriate times. In effect, you have "reset" your body's hunger clock.

The Skipper is not necessarily a chronic dieter, although the meal-skipping pattern can easily lead to chronic dieting. The Skipper may begin this pattern because of a work schedule or in an attempt to lose weight. Once the body clock is reset by proper eating, weight loss becomes possible and the symptoms of low metabolic rate disappear. The Skipper is the least complex of the three types, and the treatment can take effect very quickly, usually within three to four weeks.

CASE HISTORY: A CLOCK SET ON THE WRONG TIME

Elaine, a 34-year-old hospital intensive care nurse, was 5 feet 4 inches tall and weighed 142 pounds. She had worked days for several years, then she began a rotating shift—three weeks of nights, followed by three weeks of days, followed by three weeks of evenings, and so on. Although she had always struggled with her weight and had a tendency to skip meals, the change in her schedule heightened her problems. She found that when she finished work she had trouble sleeping, and the biological rhythms of her appetite changed, too. When I began treating her, Elaine reported that on the weeks she worked days, she wasn't hungry until the evening, and when she finally had a meal, she tended to overeat. During the previous several months, she had been gaining weight steadily.

Elaine was afraid that she was losing her ability to cope and was concerned with how tired she was most of the time. "My job demands alertness," she said. "I can't afford to have so little energy."

A check of Elaine's RMR revealed that it was 12 percent lower than normal. I suspected that the real culprit was her changing schedule, which confused her body about eating and sleep patterns. I asked her to keep track of her hunger patterns and her subsequent eating during different shifts. Not surprisingly, I found that Elaine's hunger cues came *after* she began to eat—whenever that was—whether she worked days or nights. On the weeks she worked days, she tended to skip meals until the evenings, then binge.

As we demonstrated in chapter 4, starving usually leads to a tendency to binge, and Starvers are hungrier *after* they eat, instead of *before* they eat. By skipping meals throughout the day, Elaine was basically setting herself up for binging episodes when she did begin to eat.

In Elaine's situation, I felt it would be next to impossible for her to establish normal eating patterns if she continued to work irregular shifts. With her agreement, we arranged for her to return to the day shift. Then she began a strict program of three meals a day.

When she first began her three-meal-a-day program, Elaine complained that she could hardly stand to eat a full breakfast every morning. "I'm just not hungry," she said. "I have to force myself to eat." On the other hand, she said that she was just as hungry as she'd always been in the evening, even though now she was eating a full breakfast and lunch. She was also experiencing some water retention. I urged her to stick with the schedule. It took three weeks for Elaine's hunger patterns to begin to correspond with her new eating schedule. The first morning that she woke up hungry, she was so excited, she called me and said, "Guess what? I'm hungry!" By this time, Elaine was also losing water that she had retained. Because her metabolic rate had not dipped too low, it was fairly easy for Elaine to get back to normal and begin losing weight.

You can evaluate whether you are a Skipper by comparing your questionnaire answers to the following points of the Skipper profile.

YOUR DIETING HISTORY

- As a Skipper, you may or may not have a history of dieting. The meal-skipping pattern might not emerge from weight-loss attempts at all—it may be the result of your work schedule or other environmental factors. But the metabolic results are similar (though less severe) to those experienced by the Starver.

YOUR METABOLIC SCORE

- Why do you have the same metabolic symptoms as the Starver, even though you may eat enough calories during the course of a day? Your pattern of skipping meals mimics the starvation signals. During a typical day, you probably skip breakfast, eat a light lunch (or go without), and end up consuming a large percentage of your calories in the evening. Remember the meal-skipping studies we conducted at the Mayo Clinic? We found that those who skipped breakfast and/or lunch began their days with the lowest Resting Metabolic Rates. We also found that since eating itself increases the metabolic rate, meal-skippers burned fewer calories throughout the day because they weren't getting that extra "burn-off" after the meals they skipped.
- You experience some or all of the symptoms of low metabolic rate that are common to the Starver, but your symptoms are less severe. Symptoms include a general feeling of lethargy and lack of energy, dry skin and hair, puffy skin and bloating, sleep irregularities, and mild depression or "blue" moods.

YOUR EATING AND ACTIVITY PATTERNS

- You always or usually skip breakfast. In fact, you are *physically* not hungry at breakfast time.

- Because your "hunger clock" has been reset to favor night eating, you consume most of your calories then. On those occasions when you eat more food earlier in the day, you get hungry again two or three hours later.
- If meal skipping begins as an attempt to lose weight, you share the Starver's tendency to eat as little as possible during the day. What normally occurs is that you "save" calories at breakfast and again at lunch, then eat in the evening. Dieting Skippers who focus on counting calories alone will be puzzled that they are not losing weight when their total daily intake is low.
- You may binge once or twice a week, usually in the evening.

ATTITUDES THAT CONTRIBUTE TO YOUR PREDICAMENT

Like many Skippers, you may have started this pattern as a weight-control method. You began skipping meals to control your calorie intake but were frustrated by your lack of progress.

Psychologically, it's very important for you to exercise control over your environment—and you are proud of your ability to discipline yourself, even when your sacrifice offers no rewards.

Not every Skipper starts out as a dieter. Sometimes the pattern begins when a busy work schedule leaves you no time for lunch, or when you'd rather sleep an extra half hour than eat breakfast. You may be a night eater because you're a night or swing-shift worker. Or maybe your pattern began after a divorce or the death of a longtime partner, when your former meal patterns were broken. Recently published statistics on the elderly show that widowed men and women often undereat or skip meals because they have trouble readjusting to their new singles' schedules.

Type 3: The Stuffer

The primary characteristic of the Stuffer is that *you overeat, usually for reasons other than physiological need*. In a sense, you "live to eat," and food becomes the primary nurturing factor in your life. Unlike the Starver, you do not necessarily binge. Rather, you eat constantly and you plan your life around food.

CASE HISTORY: THE COMPULSION TO EAT

Tom, a burly man of 37, referred to himself as a compulsive eater and told me it felt as though he had a switch in his brain that flicked on and filled him with an overwhelming desire for food, even when he didn't feel hungry. At the time he came to the clinic, he was carrying 330 pounds on his 6-foot-2-inch frame.

When I examined him, I found that Tom had many of the classic medical conditions that obese Stuffers share—shortness of breath, rapid pulse, high blood pressure, high blood sugar, high blood triglycerides, and high cholesterol.

Being big was common in Tom's family. His father had been a large man and both his older brother and younger sister were overweight. As often happens in families where people have a genetic propensity to be bigger than average, there was a strong focus on dieting. Ironically, if Tom had never dieted, he would have grown into a large but healthy adult and would probably have weighed around 220 pounds. But throughout his life he had alternated starvation diets with periods of extreme overeating. Eventually, dieting took its toll. Not only did he gain more weight each time he went off a diet than he had lost initially, but he began to feel that efforts to control his weight were futile.

When he first came to me, Tom described himself as having no control over food. "Once I start eating, I can't stop," was the way he described it. He wondered if he should have his jaw wired shut or try one of the popular fasting programs. He was desperate enough to try anything. He felt deeply ashamed that he couldn't control his eating, and he was so embarrassed about his size that he had started isolating himself. Lonely and bored, he only ate more.

Tom's case was complex because, over time, his eating had become symptomatic of a range of psychological and behavioral problems that needed to be addressed in conjunction with his physical health. This is where traditional diet programs are usually found lacking. They reinforce all the negatives about being obese and fail to lend the proper psychological or behavioral support that a person like Tom needs. Any weight-loss endeavor that sets up false circumstances to generate weight loss—such as jaw wiring, liquid diets, or fasting—bypasses the human circumstances that are integral to the weight problem. No wonder so many of these programs fail in the long term. With a person like Tom, who believes he has an addiction to food, it may be possible to get his weight down by eliminating food. But what happens when Tom is placed back in a normal situation? He panics because he still doesn't know how to handle normal eating.

The first priority in Tom's treatment was to get some of his weight off quickly to relieve his medical problems. I put him on an initial high-carbohydrate diet of 1,500 calories daily (900 calories less than his Resting Metabolic Rate) for six weeks to relieve his diabetes and lower his triglycerides and blood pressure. I also started him on an exercise program that involved brisk walking every day—beginning with ten minutes and gradually working up to twenty minutes, then increasing in intensity.

Like most overeaters, Tom was highly motivated to work and fared well with a program that demanded his participation on many levels. In addition to diet and exercise, I asked him to keep a diary and record what he ate, how much he exercised, and a description of what he was feeling when he had a "compulsion" to eat. Tom's diary became quite a document! (He keeps it to this day, even though he is no longer in the program.)

After six weeks, Tom had lost 20 pounds and his medical symptoms were sufficiently relieved that I could raise him to 2,400 calories daily to encourage a more gradual weight loss. It seemed like a lot of calories to Tom, but for a man of his size, it was only the number he burned at rest. Accompanied by regular exercise, he would be able to lose weight at a level of 1 to 2 pounds per week.

Tom's weight loss was slow but steady. After a year and a half, he had reduced to 215 pounds, the lowest his weight had ever been. During that time he had not been starving, so his compulsion to eat had disappeared. His entire demeanor had changed to reflect a new self-confidence forged out of his success. No longer did he feel that he was running on a treadmill. For the first time, he felt in control.

Tom looked fit and healthy at 215 pounds. His blood sugar, triglycerides, cholesterol, and blood pressure were normal. I told him it was time for him to stop losing weight and concentrate on increasing his activity and fitness. He resisted—he wanted to get down to 190 pounds.

"Why?" I asked him. "You're at a healthy weight. You look good, you feel good. You're a big man, Tom. If you try to be something else, you're going to be back in the same boat you were in before."

He agreed reluctantly, but I could see he wasn't convinced. The power of the scale is so great! But now, five years later, Tom has maintained his healthy weight, which is more than he could have said if he had turned to yet another quick weight-loss diet to reach an ideal that was totally outside his genetic realm.

*   *   *

You can evaluate whether you are a Stuffer by comparing your questionnaire answers to the following points of the Stuffer profile.

YOUR DIETING HISTORY

- You are now a Stuffer, but you may once have been a Starver. A focus on food—whether it is on eating it or on not eating it—can lead to the development of a compulsion to eat. Sometimes deprivation leads to a disproportionate craving for food. If you are a former Starver, you may have also become a Stuffer because you believed you had finally lost the battle to control your weight. You may have tried many low-calorie diets, but have never lasted on them long enough to lower your metabolic rate.
- Some Stuffers are genetically larger than average. There is a family history of weight problems that are symptomatic of both Starvers and Stuffers.

YOUR METABOLIC SCORE

- You often feel warmer than other people; you sweat a lot and have moist skin. This is caused by your body working overtime to metabolize and store the excess calories you consume.
- You have frequent bowel movements.
- Your pulse is high (usually above 90) and you have high blood pressure and experience shortness of breath with mild exercise or exertion. These are very dangerous symptoms. Stuffers are more likely to be candidates for heart attacks, diabetes, and other serious medical conditions.
- You experience depression. This manifests itself in mood swings, irritability, and a general feeling of being unwell.

YOUR EATING AND
ACTIVITY PATTERNS

- You overeat as a result of psychological, rather than biological, cues; your hunger is mobilized by stress, anger, boredom, loneliness, excitement, or any other strong emotional reaction. You no longer recognize what it feels like to be physically hungry.
- You isolate yourself from others and overeat when you are alone, using food as a substitute for the closeness you are lacking. There are particular foods that give you more comfort than others.
- You eat (or think about eating) all day long. Stuffers do not necessarily gorge themselves when they eat. They commonly eat "seconds" and frequent snacks. Leisure activities like reading a book or watching TV are usually accompanied by food.
- It is uncommon for you to engage in regular forms of exercise. Physical activity counters the Stuffing urge, blunting the cravings. Exercise and Stuffing are rarely consistent with each other.

ATTITUDES THAT CONTRIBUTE
TO YOUR PREDICAMENT

The profile of the Stuffer is the most complex of the three, since psychological motivations for eating are significantly more difficult to address than biological cues. The psychological background is an individual matter—some Stuffers desire escape, others acceptance. It is not uncommon for Stuffers to remain fat in order to create a barrier between themselves and the rest of the world—and particularly to avoid intimate encounters.

Some Stuffers come from troubled homes and learned from an early age that food could serve as a surrogate for love, offering a physical fullness that wasn't present emotionally. There is evidence that certain foods chemically provide a tranquilizing effect; it is these foods to which the Stuffer is most drawn.

A Stuffer's depression is usually due to much more than the consequences of metabolic imbalance. It's a complex bag of guilt, defensiveness, unhappiness, and isolation. On one hand, you feel guilty when you overeat. But if you're challenged, you tend to become defensive and take a posture of, "It's my life . . . get off my back!" You may resent others because their lives seem less lonely than yours, or you may blame them for your problem ("How can I lose weight when you keep so much food in the house?").

Some Stuffers join "fat pride" organizations for the wrong reasons: They participate as an act of self-justification and low self-esteem. For some, these organizations can become the catalyst for the resolution of their problems. But for others, they become a form of defiance or escape. This can become dangerous when a misdirected "fat pride" leads a Stuffer to ignore the real and present medical dangers caused by overeating.

If you began your dieting experience as a Starver, you may be particularly fragile psychologically. After all, you've declared yourself a permanent failure; the more you eat, the more distance you create between yourself and the cultural ideal you once sought to emulate.

I am not a psychiatrist or a psychologist. I usually recommend that Stuffers seek evaluation and supportive care from those professionals to supplement their diet plans. It's essential that the psychological issues get dealt with along with the physical manifestations.

A Word of Caution: These Symptoms Are Red Flags!

You should always consult a physician before starting a weight-loss program. If after you've started this program you have weight gain associated with any of the following symptoms, you must see your doctor. They may indicate conditions that require special testing and treatment.

1. Abnormal thirst or extremely dry mouth
2. Excessive or frequent urination
3. Hoarse voice not associated with a cold or bronchitis
4. (Women) Increased facial or body hair
5. Milky discharge from the breast
6. Progressively more severe headaches
7. Double vision or loss of vision
8. Unexplained fever or chills
9. Muscle wasting or weakness
10. Purple stretch marks
11. Sexual impotence
12. Hallucinations, psychosis, or other severe psychiatric disturbances

SIX

The Starver

It's time now to put the life of starving behind you and begin to view yourself as the friend and benevolent caretaker of your body, not its strict taskmaster or policeman. The thin distortion, which we discussed in chapter 2, has led you to value deprivation as a positive step toward achieving your goal. Whenever you began a diet, it was viewed as a good thing, even though each time you ended up gaining back as much as or more fat than you lost.

However, as we've seen, dieting has actually triggered your rebound weight gain. Dieting has contributed to your fatigue, depression, and other symptoms. Dieting has increased your tendency to binge. Each time you've dieted, success has been harder to achieve.

You think you have failed.

In reality, *your body has succeeded*—succeeded in adapting marvelously well to semistarvation by burning less and less and less. The task now is to get your metabolic rate back to normal so you can lose weight. To do so, it is necessary that you first start eating enough to turn off the starvation signals. Once you get enough of the right kinds of foods on the right schedule, you will be able to lose body fat without setting off your body's starvation defenses.

The challenge for you will be patience. That is why it is so important to understand what has happened to your body when you've dieted in the past, and what you can expect to happen when you go on this diet. If your past experience now makes sense, you are more likely to stick with the plan. If this does not yet make sense, go back and reread the earlier chapters. Don't proceed on blind faith. Know why you are doing what you are about to do. Success will come more easily.

This plan is quite different from those you've followed before:

- Before, you feared food as a direct challenge to your self-control. Now, you will learn to eat again. Adequate food is essential to your recovery.
- Before, you evaluated your progress by weighing yourself frequently. Now, you will identify a series of milestones along the way to your final goal, which is to live a satisfying life. Weight loss will take its place alongside your other goals. It will no longer control your life.
- Before, you resigned yourself to a cycle of weight loss and weight gain. Now, you can expect to reach your weight goal and maintain it for the rest of your life.
- Before, dieting resulted in fatigue, depression, and other side effects. Now, your eating and exercise plan will help you recover your energy, lift your spirits, and feel a greater sense of self-control.

MAKE A COMMITMENT TO TRY SOMETHING DIFFERENT

As a chronic dieter, you carry in the back of your mind the fear (whether you admit it or not) that *you're always going to be overweight.* You've already tried every diet invented by man. Some have worked temporarily; none have brought lasting success. Why should this one work?

The answer is that this diet is based on a better understanding of the factors regulating body size and body shape and how our bodies respond to deprivation. It is based on vast research and clinical studies conducted by myself and others in the field. It is the result of more than twenty years of work, not simply a fad. And I have used this approach successfully for years, treating thousands of people.

The initial six weeks of the diet are the most challenging. But they can also be the most rewarding. Right now, you may have forgotten what it's like to feel really good physically and emotionally. But as your metabolic rate returns to normal, your symptoms of fatigue and depression will disappear. This is one of the first things my patients report to me: They *feel* so much better.

However, the first six weeks can also be a struggle, and this is something we need to talk about right now. If you have a history of going on and off semistarvation diets—and this is the most common profile of the Starver—your metabolic rate may be 15 percent or more below normal. As we described earlier, when your metabolic rate is low and you begin to eat more calories, there is an initial period of water weight gain, which is called refeeding edema. The period of water weight gain is the most difficult challenge my patients face. Even those who have been educated thoroughly and have attended our group sessions still struggle with this. And why shouldn't they? This initial phase of the diet goes against all the popular notions about dieting. That's why I'm making a special point of it here—you need to be ready for it and understand its role as an essential step in reaching your permanent weight-loss goal.

It might be helpful if you think of the period of water retention as being like a savings bank. When you put your money in savings, it is not available for you to spend now, but you know you have it. In other words, it isn't the same as *not having* the money. And while it's in savings, it's performing a positive function—earning you interest. The same is true of the water weight gain that appears in the initial stage of the Starver's diet. You are in the process of losing weight—you just can't see it now. Your weight loss, like the money in savings, is not "available" to you. But the fact that you are experiencing the initial water weight gain means that the diet is working for you. You'll actually be able to cash in on the difference later.

As you struggle with this, you might also allow your mind to travel back over the many diets you've tried in the past. Remember when you could drop 5 pounds in a week? Those were the good old days, right? But I assure you that you were not dropping 5 pounds of fat—it was mostly water. And the plateau you reached after a few weeks (if you lasted on the diet long enough to reach it) was the normal biological operation of your kidneys reacting to the extreme water loss by beginning to conserve water. When you reached that plateau you may have become discouraged and concluded that the diet had stopped working. But it never *was* working.

Once you went off the diet, things only grew worse. You were gaining weight, feeling bloated, experiencing muscle aches, and feeling cold, tired, weepy, and short-tempered. This only heightened your discouragement.

Like it or not, these are scientific facts. Your choice is clear: You can continue this pattern or you can do what it takes to break it once and for all.

In this chapter, I will describe what you can expect to experience during the early stages of the diet—how you will feel and what will happen to your body. I will give you a series of milestones that will become the checkpoints that can reassure you that the appropriate changes are taking place.

The Starver's Diet Program

During the first six weeks of the diet, you will experience many changes very fast. I usually suggest that my patients begin by purchasing a notebook to keep track

of their progress. This is a very useful tool to reinforce
a sense of control.

There will be a number of tasks for you to perform
in the course of your diet. These include:

1. Determine how many calories you will need to eat
every day to raise your metabolic rate to a level that will
allow you to lose.

2. Fill out your Daily Food Chart, choosing your menus
from chapter 9, and keeping careful track of the amount
of food you've eaten and the time and circumstances.
In past diets, you kept a diary to control yourself from
eating too much. Now your diary will help you make
sure you're eating enough.

3. Check your Milestone Scale on the seventh day of
each week. This chart lists the symptoms that are common for the Starver—the symptoms that have been
interfering with your enjoyment of life *and* preventing
you from losing weight. You should feel increasingly
excited as you watch these symptoms disappear. It means
that you are finally recovering, and your years on the
weight loss/weight gain treadmill are about to end.

4. Each week, perform the Personal Awareness Exercise described in chapter 11. This will help you relate
personally to the material we discussed earlier in the
book. Recovering your metabolic balance and losing
weight are only part of the process. The Personal Awareness Exercise allows you to reflect on the larger life-
satisfaction issues that are the cornerstone of this diet.
It helps you keep your weight-loss goal in perspective as
being only one step on the road to greater life pleasure.

HOW MANY CALORIES PER DAY?

How many calories a day should you eat to lose
weight? Chronic dieters have a completely inaccurate
picture of this, for the reasons we discussed earlier.

When your body fights starvation and your kidneys start to retain water, it may appear that you gain weight on as little as 800 to 1,000 calories per day. Eventually, after long years of yo-yo dieting, you probably have no clear idea how many calories you should eat.

To determine how many calories you need to consume in order to lose, maintain, or gain weight, you must first find your Resting Metabolic Rate (RMR)—the number of calories an average person of your age, height, weight, and sex would burn at rest. You can calculate this with reasonable accuracy at home, using the following method.

The average, moderately active person burns about 30 percent more calories per day than his or her RMR. But the Starver, with a low metabolic rate, may be burning as little as 15 to 30 percent below normal. For this reason, you must consume *more* calories during the first six weeks of your program to regain metabolic balance.

The following equation will tell you how many calories you must eat during the first six weeks. **Do not deviate from this amount.**

WOMEN:

1. Begin with a base of 655 calories   <u> 655 </u>
2. Multiply your weight (in pounds) × 4.3 <u>   </u>
3. Multiply your height (in inches) × 4.7 <u>   </u>
4. Add together the totals from #1, #2, and #3   <u>   </u>
5. Multiply your age × 4.7   <u>   </u>
6. Subtract result of #5 from total of #4   <u>   </u> *Your normal RMR*
7. Multiply the result of #6 × 1.1   <u>   </u>
8. Round off #7 to the nearest 100   <u>   </u> *Your daily calories*

Sample

Woman: 140 pounds/ 5'3"/age 39

1. Base calories	655
2. 140 (pounds) × 4.3	602
3. 63 (inches) × 4.7	296

4. 1+2+3	1553	
5. 39 (years) × 4.7	183	
6. #4 − #5	1370	*Normal RMR*
7. 1370 × 1.1	1507	
8. Rounded off	1500	*Daily calories*

MEN:

1. Begin with a base of 66 calories	66	
2. Multiply your weight (in pounds) × 6.3	___	
3. Multiply your height (in inches) × 12.7	___	
4. Add together the totals from #1, #2, and #3	___	
5. Multiply your age × 6.8	___	
6. Subtract result of #5 from total of #4	___	*Your normal RMR*
7. Multiply the result of #6 × 1.1	___	
8. Round off #7 to the nearest 100	___	*Your daily calories*

Sample

Man: 180 pounds/5′9″/age 40

1. Base calories	66	
2. 180 (pounds) × 6.3	1134	
3. 69 (inches) × 12.7	876	
4. 1+2+3	2076	
5. 40 (years) × 6.8	272	
6. #4 − #5	1804	*Normal RMR*
7. 1804 × 1.1	1984	
8. Rounded off	2000	*Daily calories*

HOW TO EAT

Follow these eating guidelines exactly as they are stated. Your menus, recipes, and food plans appear in chapter 9.

Rule 1: Do not deviate from the number of calories you must eat daily, based on your calculation. This number appears high to the Starver, but *you cannot achieve permanent weight loss unless you eat this amount during the first six weeks.*

Rule 2: Use the menu plans and food lists to construct your weekly diet. Do not substitute foods that are not listed. The menu plans are designed to supply the right balance of complex carbohydrates, protein, and fat. If you have been "trained" in the low-carbohydrate school of weight loss, it will seem strange to be eating so many complex carbohydrates. Carbohydrate deprivation has led to many of your problems, including water retention. Eating enough complex carbohydrates is the best way to restore metabolic balance and lose weight long term.

Rule 3: Consume no alcohol during the first six weeks. Alcohol can set off the urge to binge. Do not drink more than the two cups of caffeinated coffee or tea allowed each day.

Rule 4: Eat three meals each day, at *the same hours each day*. Consume approximately the same number of calories during each meal, or at least 25 percent of daily calories at any given meal.

Rule 5: Do not eat any snacks between meals or save food from meals to eat later as snacks. You must eat all your food at the three mealtimes. (A cup of hot decaffeinated tea is a good way to lift your energy level and cut your hunger between meals.)

Rule 6: Do not begin exercising until your metabolic rate has reached a normal level. Exercise prior to that point will only delay your recovery.

THE MILESTONE SCALE

At the end of each week, mark your improvements on the Milestone Scale. This scale represents the reliable disappearance of the symptoms you have been suffering as a result of your low metabolic rate. Typically, the symptoms disappear in the order in which they're listed, although there's some variation from person to person. (Refer to chapter 5 for instructions on how to test for water retention and pulse rate.)

STOP AND EVALUATE AFTER SIX WEEKS

As we have said before, every dieter is different. The time it takes your metabolic rate to return to normal will depend on your history of starving and on how much below normal it is. I have seen people with metabolic rates of 5 to 10 percent below normal reach a normal metabolic rate within three weeks; others, whose metabolic rates had slowed down to a level of 20 percent or more below normal, have taken as long as three months to reach a normal point. If you are one of the latter, I urge you not to get discouraged and give up. You *are* on the way to achieving your goal, even if it doesn't seem that way.

Rather than worry because you are still retaining water, concentrate on the other milestones that you crossed during the first six weeks. These milestones mean a lot to your long-term success. And you should be *feeling* much better.

Check your progress by answering the following questions:

1. You no longer feel cold when others feel comfortable. ____YES ____NO
2. Your skin is no longer so dry. ____YES ____NO
3. You're no longer constipated. ____YES ____NO
4. Your lightheadedness has ceased. ____YES ____NO
5. You are able to eat normally, without fighting the urge to binge. ____YES ____NO
6. Your resting pulse rate has increased. ____YES ____NO
7. You sleep normally and wake up refreshed. ____YES ____NO
8. Your moods are more stable— you've begun to lose the blues. ____YES ____NO
9. You've started losing some of the water you've retained. ____YES ____NO
10. You've stopped feeling bloated after eating. ____YES ____NO

DIET MILESTONE SCALE

	WK 1	WK 2	WK 3	WK 4	WK 5	WK 6
1. Lightheadedness when you stand						
2. Intolerance to cold						
3. Tired when you wake up						
4. Little energy during the day						
5. Dry skin						
6. Constipation						
7. Frequent feelings of depression						
8. Abdominal cramps and bloating after eating						
9. Water retention						
10. Urge to binge when you eat						

TOTAL:
Resting pulse rate:
(Normal: between 60 and 90)

Instructions: Check your milestones on the seventh day of each week. Put a check after each symptom that's still present. Then add the total number. By the third week, several of your symptoms should be gone and you'll be feeling much better.

At the end of six weeks, most people will have lost many of these symptoms. Keep tracking your milestones regularly until all of your symptoms have gone—in particular, the water retention caused by refeeding edema.

If you are still suffering from severe symptoms of a low metabolic rate after six weeks, check to make sure that you have been following the instructions exactly as they are stated:

- Are you eating enough calories?
- Are you following the menus and food lists?
- Have you been skipping any meals?
- Have you been snacking between meals?
- Have you been refraining from exercise?

Any break with the rules may lead to problems. Make sure that you have followed each rule correctly. Then, if you find no cause for your lack of progress, see your doctor again. Your problem might be due to a previously undetected thyroid condition or to other factors that require medical supervision.

THE NEXT PHASE

Once your metabolic rate has been restored to a level point, you can move on to the next phase of your diet. During this phase:

1. You will start a program of moderate exercise, as outlined in chapter 10, and begin keeping an exercise record.

2. You will reduce your calorie intake to normal RMR, and you will begin to be able to calculate more reliably how much weight you can expect to lose. Follow these steps to project your weight loss, and repeat them every six weeks as needed until you reach your goal:

A. Reweigh yourself and measure your waist/hip ratio, according to the instructions in chapter 5.

B. Return to the RMR/calorie measurement earlier in this chapter. You may now revise your intake to a lower level. To do this, eliminate step 7. Your new calorie allotment is the result from step 6, rounded off. (For example, in the sample used for women, the new allowance is 1,370 calories, rounded off to 1,400 calories.)

C. To calculate approximately how much fat you will lose (not counting the additional benefits of your exercise program) during a six-week period, use this equation:

a) Divide your daily calories by 3 ____

b) Multiply the result × 42 (the number of days in six weeks) ____

c) Divide the result by 3500 (the number of calories per pound of fat) ____

Sample

Daily Calories: 1500

1500 divided by 3	=	500
500 × 42	=	21,000
21,000 divided by 3500	=	6*

*pound loss from eating, not including exercise

SEVEN

The Skipper

Your initial task will be to turn your hunger clock back to normal. Because you probably consume most of your calories late in the day, your appetite has reset itself to this pattern. Now you suffer from a lowered metabolic rate, difficulty in losing weight, and an inability to recognize genuine physical hunger signals.

Since your metabolic rate is only 5 to 10 percent below normal, it won't take long for you to reach stability. Your real challenge will be to modify your eating patterns sufficiently to reset your clock—and then continue to maintain a normal meal schedule.

How quickly you return to normal will depend, in large part, on your reasons for skipping meals. If you are really a budding Starver, you will need more time to put your eating and weight in perspective. If it is your work schedule that is at odds with regular eating patterns, you will have less trouble emotionally, but perhaps more trouble practically.

Although your metabolic imbalance is not severe, it is still interfering with your energy, your general mood, and your ability to lose weight. And it will become progressively worse. You're lucky that you don't yet have severe problems. Take advantage of this opportunity to get yourself back on track.

This chapter will outline your program—a modified form of the Starver's diet plan, with particular emphasis on your eating patterns. Before you begin, reread chapter 6 to familiarize yourself with the Starver's plan. You may identify with the Starver in many ways—even though your plight is less serious at this time. You may be able to stabilize in a very short time—as little as three weeks.

In this chapter, I will describe what you can expect to experience during the early stages of the diet—how you will feel and what will happen to your body. You will also be given a "Hunger Scale" to help track your progress in normalizing your hunger signals, and a series of milestones that will be the checkpoints to reassure you that the appropriate changes are taking place. I suggest that you buy a notebook to keep track of your progress.

The Skipper's Diet Program

During the first six weeks of the diet, you will have four tasks:

1. Determine how many calories you will need to eat every day to raise your metabolic rate to a level that will allow you to lose weight more easily.

2. Fill out your Daily Food Chart, choosing your menus from chapter 9, and keeping careful track of the amount of food you've eaten, as well as the time and circumstances. In past diets, you kept a diary to control yourself from eating too much. Now your diary will help you make sure you're eating enough at each meal.

3. Check your Milestone Scale on the seventh day of each week. This chart lists the symptoms that are common for the Skipper—the symptoms that have been interfering with your enjoyment of life *and* preventing you from losing weight. You should feel increasingly excited as you watch these symptoms disappear. It means that you are getting back to normal.

4. Each week, perform the Personal Awareness Exercise described in chapter 11. This will help you relate personally to the material we discussed earlier in the book. Recovering your metabolic balance and losing weight are only part of the process. The Personal Awareness Exercise allows you to reflect on the larger life-satisfaction issues that are the cornerstone of this diet. It helps you keep your weight-loss goal in perspective as being only one step on the road to greater life pleasure.

BEFORE YOU BEGIN

Use your notebook to record your eating patterns for one full week. Don't make any changes in your habits—just write down exactly what you eat, the number of calories, and the time of day. Also check the times you felt hungry, using the diary below.

HUNGER DIARY

	M	T	W	TH	F	S	S
6:00 A.M.							
7:00 A.M.							
8:00 A.M.							
9:00 A.M.							
10:00 A.M.							
11:00 A.M.							
12:00 noon							
1:00 P.M.							
2:00 P.M.							
3:00 P.M.							
4:00 P.M.							

	M	**T**	**W**	**TH**	**F**	**S**	**S**
5:00 P.M.							
6:00 P.M.							
7:00 P.M.							
8:00 P.M.							
9:00 P.M.							
10:00 P.M.							
11:00 P.M.							
12:00 mid							

Put a check beside the times each day you feel hungry or have the urge to eat.

At the end of the week, evaluate your results:

1. How many calories did you eat each day before noon? How many calories did you eat each day between noon and 6:00 P.M.? How many calories did you eat each day after 6:00 P.M.?

2. How many meals did you skip each day? What was your total of skipped meals during the week?

3. Track the checkmarks on your hunger scale. What times of day did they frequently appear? Were there large periods of time when you did not feel hungry? Were there periods when you felt particularly hungry?

This evaluation of your current patterns will give you an idea of where you're off track—how your body has adjusted to inappropriate patterns. By following the diet rules, you will restore normal hunger patterns, which is the first step in your recovery.

HOW MANY CALORIES PER DAY?

How many calories a day should you eat to lose weight? Right now, your eating pattern is making it hard for you to lose, even on very low-calorie diets. Chances are, while you're skipping meals you are also not eating enough. During the first six weeks, you will need to eat a little more than you are used to eating on previous diets.

To determine how many calories you need to consume, you must first find your Resting Metabolic Rate (RMR)—the number of calories an average person of your age, height, weight, and sex would burn at rest. You can calculate this with reasonable accuracy at home, using the following method.

The average, moderately active person burns about 30 percent more calories per day than his or her RMR. But the Skipper is probably burning about 5 to 10 percent fewer calories than normal. By consuming only the number of calories a normal person burns at rest, you will be able to restore your metabolic balance and lose weight. This equation will tell you how many calories you need. **Do not deviate from this amount.**

WOMEN:

1. Begin with a base of 655 calories   655
2. Multiply your weight (in pounds) × 4.3   ____
3. Multiply your height (in inches) × 4.7   ____
4. Add together the totals from #1, #2, and #3   ____
5. Multiply your age × 4.7   ____
6. Subtract result of #5 from total of #4   ____ *Your normal RMR*
7. Round off #6 to the nearest 100   ____ *Your daily calories*

Sample

Woman: 140 pounds/5'3"/age 39

1. Base calories	655
2. 140 (pounds) × 4.3	602
3. 63 (inches) × 4.7	296
4. 1 + 2 + 3	1553
5. 39 (years) × 4.7	183
6. #4 − #5	1370 *Normal RMR*
7. Rounded off	1400 *Daily Calories*

MEN:

1. Begin with a base of 66 calories   <u>66</u>
2. Multiply your weight (in pounds) × 6.3   ____
3. Multiply your height (in inches) × 12.7   ____
4. Add together the totals from #1, #2, and #3   ____
5. Multiply your age × 6.8   ____
6. Subtract the result of #5 from total of #4   ____ *Your normal RMR*
7. Round off #6 to the nearest 100   ____ *Your daily calories*

Sample

Man: 180 pounds/5′9″/age 40

1. Base calories	66
2. 180 (pounds) × 6.3	1134
3. 69 (inches) × 12.7	876
4. 1+2+3	2076
5. 40 (years) × 6.8	272
6. #4 − #5	1804 *Normal RMR*
7. Rounded off	1800 *Daily calories*

HOW TO EAT

Follow these eating guidelines exactly as they are stated. Your menus, recipes, and food plans appear in chapter 9.

Rule 1: Do not deviate from the number of calories you must eat daily, based on your calculation. This is the only way your metabolic rate will return to normal.

Rule 2: Follow the menu plans and food lists to construct your weekly diet. Do not substitute foods that are not listed. The menu plans are designed to supply the right balance of complex carbohydrates, protein, and fat. If you have been "trained" in the low-carbohydrate school of weight loss, it will seem strange to be eating so many complex carbohydrates. Carbohydrate deprivation has led to many of your problems, including water retention. Eating enough complex carbohydrates is the best way to restore metabolic balance and lose weight.

Rule 3: Consume no alcohol during the first six weeks. Alcohol can set off the urge to binge. Do not drink more than the two cups of caffeinated coffee allowed each day, and drink them in the morning, not in the evening.

Rule 4: Eat three meals each day, scheduled at *the same hours each day*. Consume approximately the same number of calories during each meal, or at least 25 percent of your calories at any given meal. In the beginning, you will not feel physically hungry at breakfast. You may have to force yourself to eat. But follow the plan and eventually you will be hungry at appropriate times.

Rule 5: Do not eat any snacks between meals or save food from meals to eat later. You must eat all your food during the three mealtimes. You will be much more successful resetting your hunger clock if you don't confuse your body with unscheduled eating. (A cup of hot decaffeinated tea is a good way to lift your energy level and cut your hunger between meals.)

Rule 6: Do not begin exercising until your metabolic rate has reached normal. Exercise prior to that point will only sabotage your progress.

THE MILESTONE SCALE

At the end of each week, mark your improvements on the Milestone Scale (see page 108). This scale represents the predicted disappearance of the symptoms you have been suffering as a result of a lowered metabolic rate and a confused hunger clock. (Refer to chapter 5 for instructions on how to test for water retention and pulse rate.)

STOP AND EVALUATE
AFTER SIX WEEKS

By the end of six weeks, the Skipper should have a normal hunger pattern, normal metabolic rate, feel better, and be losing weight. Many Skippers get back to normal within the first three weeks, but don't worry if it has taken you a little longer. Remember: Not every dieter is alike!

It is now time to stop and review the progress you have made, using the checklist from your Milestone Scale. Answer the following questions True or False to confirm your current status:

1. You are hungry before breakfast.   ____T ____F
2. You are less hungry between meals
   and in the evening.   ____T ____F
3. You're no longer constipated.   ____T ____F
4. You are able to eat normally, with-
   out fighting the urge to binge.   ____T ____F
5. Your resting pulse rate has
   increased.   ____T ____F
6. Your skin is not dry.   ____T ____F
7. You sleep normally and wake up
   refreshed.   ____T ____F
8. Your moods are more stable—
   you've begun to lose the blues.   ____T ____F
9. You've lost or have started losing
   the water you retained.   ____T ____F
10. You've stopped feeling bloated af-
    ter eating.   ____T ____F

At the end of six weeks you will have lost all or nearly all of your symptoms and will be able to begin the next phase of your diet.

DIET MILESTONE SCALE

	WK 1	WK 2	WK 3	WK 4	WK 5	WK 6
1. Not hungry before breakfast						
2. Hungry in the late afternoon						
3. Urge to eat after dinner						
4. Urge to binge at least once a week						
5. Mild intolerance to cold						
6. Occasional constipation						
7. Drier than normal skin						
8. Mild water retention and bloating after eating						
9. General feeling of low energy						
10. Moodiness and mild depression						

TOTAL:
Resting pulse rate:
(Normal: between 60 and 90)

Instructions: Check your milestones on the seventh day of each week. Put a check after each symptom that's still present. Then add the total number. By the third week, most or all of your symptoms should be gone and you'll be feeling much better.

Your pulse may be only slightly lower than normal, in the low to middle 70s. Monitor your pulse weekly as it rises to a normal rate.

If, after six weeks, you are still struggling with hunger at inappropriate times, check to make sure that you have been following the instructions exactly as they are stated:

- Are you eating enough calories at each meal?
- Are you following the menus and food lists?
- Have you been snacking between meals?
- Are you eating each of your three meals within one hour of its designated time?
- Have you been refraining from exercise?

Any break with the rules may lead to problems. Make sure that you have followed each rule correctly. Then, if you find no cause for your lack of progress, see your doctor again. Your problem might be due to other factors that require medical attention.

THE NEXT PHASE

Once your appetite and metabolic rate have been restored to a level point, you can move on to the next phase of your diet. During this phase:

1. You will begin a program of moderate exercise, as outlined in chapter 10, and begin keeping an exercise record.

2. You will maintain your calorie intake at the same level, and you will begin to be able to calculate more reliably how much weight you can expect to lose. Follow these steps to project your weight loss, and repeat them every six weeks as needed until you reach your goal:

A. Reweigh yourself and measure your waist/hip ratio, according to the instructions in chapter 5.

B. To calculate approximately how much weight you will lose (not counting the additional benefits of your exercise program) during a six-week period, use this equation:
  a) Divide your daily calories by 3   _____
  b) Multiply the result × 42
     (the number of days in 6 weeks)   _____
  c) Divide the result by 3500
     (the number of calories per
     pound of fat)   _____

Sample

Daily Calories: 1500

1500 divided by 3   =   500
500 × 42   =   21,000
21,000 divided by 3500   =   6*

*pound loss from eating, not including exercise

EIGHT

The Stuffer

Your overeating, which has raised your metabolic rate and increased your risk for health problems, makes your plight more dangerous than that of the other types of dieters. In addition, the psychological factors (loneliness, boredom, stress, excitement, etc.) that serve as triggers for your eating increase the complexity of your dilemma.

> While you should always consult a physician before starting a weight-loss program, if you are severely overweight, and especially if you have any medical conditions, it is absolutely essential to consult your doctor before you start this diet. A complete examination is advisable to measure your blood sugar, cholesterol and triglycerides, and blood pressure—plus an electrocardiogram, if you are over 40 years of age.

Because your metabolic rate is somewhat higher than average, you will be able to lose weight more rapidly than either the Starver or the Skipper. However, if you have gone on low-calorie diets before and have lost weight rapidly, you might find that now you'll lose somewhat more slowly than you did in the past; you will not be starving as you've done before.

As you progress on the diet, you will begin to experience dramatic changes in the way you feel:

- Before, you believed that you *needed* food for psychological nurturing. Now, you will begin to appreciate food for its physiological benefits.
- Before, you secretly negated your right to have the simple pleasures others take for granted. Now, you will discover a new source of pride in who you are.
- Before, you classified yourself as a "hopeless case," doomed to be overweight. Indeed, you may even have become stoically resigned to your depression and weight-related medical conditions. Now, you will find that you are every bit as deserving of personal happiness as thin people are. And you are capable of achieving it.
- Before, you felt guilty every time you ate. Now, you will learn to manage your eating and activity patterns; your context will change from a moral one ("food is bad") to an objectified goal of achieving appropriate and healthy weight.
- Before, you allowed food to control you. Now, *you* will control your eating and your life.

MAKE A COMMITMENT TO TRY SOMETHING NEW

You may believe (deep down) that there is no hope left for you. That's because you think your overeating is the result of uncontrollable urges that cannot be changed. But this diet *will* work if you have the patience to try it. It is based on a better understanding of the causes of and cures for chronic obesity, from the vast research and clinical studies conducted by myself and others in the field. It is the result of more than twenty years of work, not simply a quick gimmick. And I have used this approach successfully for years, treating thousands of people.

The initial six-week period is the most challenging. It may also be the most rewarding. Right now, you may have forgotten what it's like to *feel* really good—physically and mentally. As your metabolic rate returns to normal, your symptoms will begin to disappear and you will find that you are happier and more secure, even while you are on the diet. These improvements should be viewed as very important signs of success. They indicate that the diet is working. And you will not feel as though you are being deprived.

In this chapter, I will describe what you can expect to experience during this six-week period—how you will feel and what will happen to your body. These milestones will become the checkpoints in your program and will reassure you that the appropriate metabolic changes are taking place as you lose weight.

It is very important that you keep a diary of your progress, so before you start, buy a notebook for this purpose. Then evaluate your eating patterns according to the method described below.

BEFORE YOU BEGIN

Set aside one week to record your eating behavior. Write down the following in your notebook:

1. Each time you eat.
2. What you eat.
3. How much you eat.
4. Where you are and whom you're with when you eat.
5. What emotional state you're in when you eat.

Evaluate the patterns of the week:

- How many times was your eating tied to an emotion like frustration, anger, loneliness, or boredom?
- On those occasions, did it make you feel better or worse to have eaten?
- Do you see a pattern that might help you control these triggers? For example, do you overeat when

• you are in certain settings or with particular people? Do you overeat more on weekends? Find the patterns and make a commitment to reduce those circumstances on a long-term basis.

The Stuffer's Diet Program

During the first six weeks, you will be concentrating on losing weight a little more rapidly than you will be losing over the long term, to bring your metabolic rate back down to normal and avoid some of the health hazards associated with obesity and high metabolic rate. You will have four primary tasks:

1. Determine how many calories you will eat every day. In the beginning, your calorie level will be lower to allow you to lose weight more quickly. Once your metabolic rate is down, your calorie allowance will be increased.

2. Fill out your Daily Food Chart, choosing your menus from chapter 9, and keeping careful track of the amount of food you've eaten, as well as the time and circumstances. Since your pattern has been to eat often throughout the day, keeping a record will help you shift your patterns.

3. Check your Milestone Scale on the seventh day of each week. This chart lists the symptoms that are common for the Stuffer—the symptoms that have been interfering with your enjoyment of life, preventing you from losing weight, and indicating that you are at increased risk for illness. You should feel increasingly excited as you watch these symptoms disappear. Your physical health and well-being will improve dramatically, and you'll begin to feel more secure and at ease with your life.

4. Each week, perform the Personal Awareness Exercise described in chapter 11. This will help you relate personally to the material we discussed earlier in the book. It will also reveal an important fact you need to hear: You are not a failure. You are not to blame for your predicament. Self-awareness will begin to chip away at the layers of defense you have built up over the years and restore your confidence in yourself and your future. It will also allow you to place your weight and weight loss in perspective, as only one step on the road to greater life satisfaction.

HOW MANY CALORIES PER DAY?

How many calories a day should you eat to lose weight? If you are overeating, you may no longer know how much you consume. Refer to the analysis you did for one week to find out how many calories you've been consuming during an average day. Since your hunger signals are not operating properly, you have trouble knowing when you've had enough to eat.

To determine how many calories you need to lose weight, you must first find your Resting Metabolic Rate (RMR)—the number of calories an average person of your age, height, weight, and sex would burn at rest. You can calculate this with reasonable accuracy at home, using the following method.

The average, moderately active person burns about 30 percent more calories per day than the RMR. But the Stuffer, with a high metabolic rate, burns calories much faster—maybe as much as 30 percent above normal. Your body works overtime to metabolize and store the excess food you are consuming. Unlike the Starver, who needs to eat *more* calories to lose, you must eat *fewer* calories than the average person of your age, sex, height, and weight would burn at rest.

The following equation will tell you how many calories you must eat during the first six weeks. **Do not deviate from this amount.**

WOMEN:

1. Begin with a base of 655 calories   655
2. Multiply your weight (in pounds) × 4.3   ____
3. Multiply your height (in inches) × 4.7   ____
4. Add together the totals from #1, #2,
   and #3   ____
5. Multiply your age × 4.7   ____
6. Subtract result of #5 from total   *Your*
   of #4   ____ *normal RMR*
7. Multiply the result of #6 × .9   ____
8. Round off to the nearest 100   ____ *Your*
                                                   daily calories

Sample

Woman: 160 pounds/5′3″/age 39
1. Base calories   655
2. 160 (pounds) × 4.3   688
3. 63 (inches) × 4.7   296
4. 1+2+3   1639
5. 39 (years) × 4.7   183
6. #4−#5   1456 *Normal RMR*
7. 1456× .9   1310
8. Rounded off   1300 *Daily calories*

MEN:

1. Begin with a base of 66 calories   66
2. Multiply your weight (in pounds) × 6.3   ____
3. Multiply your height (in inches) × 12.7   ____
4. Add together the totals from #1, #2,
   and #3   ____
5. Multiply your age × 6.8   ____
6. Subtract the result of #5 from total   *Your*
   of #4   ____ *normal RMR*
7. Multiply the result of #6 × .9   ____
8. Round off to the nearest 100   ____ *Your*
                                                   daily calories

Sample

Man: 180 pounds/5'9"/age 40

1. Base calories   66
2. 220 (pounds) × 6.3   1386
3. 69 (inches) × 12.7   876
4. 1 + 2 + 3   2328
5. 40 (years) × 6.8   272
6. #4 − #5   2056 *Normal RMR*
7. 2056 × .9   1850
8. Rounded off   1900 *Daily calories*

HOW TO EAT

These rules are the guiding principles for the first six weeks of the Stuffer's diet plan. Follow them exactly as they are stated:

Rule 1: Do not deviate from the number of calories you must eat daily, based on your calculation. This is the number of calories that will allow you to lose weight quickly during the first six weeks and stabilize down your metabolic rate.

Rule 2: Follow the menu plans and food lists in chapter 9, and do not substitute foods that are not listed. The menu plans are designed to supply the right balance of complex carbohydrates, protein, and fat.

Rule 3: Consume no alcohol during the first six weeks. Do not drink more than the two cups of caffeinated coffee allowed each day. Do not eat sugar or sugar substitutes, since there is some evidence that the consumption of sweets leads to a craving for fat. (It has been shown that a "sweet tooth" may really be a "fat tooth" in overweight people.)

Rule 4: Eat three meals every day, scheduled at *the same hours each day*. Consume approximately the same number of calories during each meal, or at least 25 percent of daily calories at any given meal. Decide from the outset that you will eat only at these three times.

Making this decision now will save you from having to remake it every time you feel the urge to eat.

Rule 5: Eat every meal sitting down at the table. Serve your food in the kitchen, putting exactly the amount of food on your plate that you will be eating. Do not do anything else (read, watch TV, etc.) while you are eating.

Rule 6: Do not eat any snacks between meals or save food from meals to eat later. Don't negotiate with this rule. Snacks won't satisfy you; they will only make you feel more hungry.

Rule 7: Don't stock food in the house that is not on your diet. Ask your family to cooperate. If you expose yourself to foods you're not permitted, you'll expend a lot more psychic energy trying to resist them.

Rule 8: Schedule your activity program as outlined in chapter 10. This will help you in three ways: You'll lose weight faster, you'll feel better about yourself right away, and you'll have a positive action to replace inappropriate eating.

THE MILESTONE SCALE

The weekly Milestone Scale will give you a way to track the predicted disappearance of the symptoms you have been suffering as a result of your overeating. Metabolic imbalance has been the cause of many of your problems. However, be aware that your problems have been more than biological; they have been psychological and emotional, too. While you will feel better and lose weight in a more reliable, long-term fashion when your metabolic rate is normal, it is not the complete answer. (Refer to chapter 5 for instructions on how to test for your pulse rate.)

STOP AND EVALUATE
AFTER SIX WEEKS

During each of the first six weeks, you were able to track the improvement of your symptoms. At the end of six weeks, you should be within 10 percent of your normal metabolic rate. You may have crossed the line during the fourth or fifth week. Not only do you *feel* better and appear more vigorous and healthy, you are burning calories at a normal rate and losing fat, not just water.

It is now time to stop and review the progress you have made, using the checklist from your Diet Milestone Scale. Answer the following questions True or False to confirm your current status:

1. You don't feel too warm when others are comfortable with the temperature.   ___T ___F
2. You no longer sweat so much or have moist skin.   ___T ___F
3. You're not overly thirsty.   ___T ___F
4. Your bowel functions are more regular.   ___T ___F
5. You don't get short of breath with mild exertion.   ___T ___F
6. You're not troubled by a frequent urge to eat.   ___T ___F
7. You've stopped snoring excessively.   ___T ___F
8. You begin to feel hungry at mealtime.   ___T ___F
9. You have more energy during the day. You don't get drowsy.   ___T ___F
10. Your mood is more "even." You don't experience so many emotional ups and downs.   ___T ___F

DIET MILESTONE SCALE

	WK 1	WK 2	WK 3	WK 4	WK 5	WK 6
1. Intolerance to heat						
2. Sweaty, moist skin						
3. Increased thirst without increase in urination						
4. Frequent bowel movements						
5. Shortness of breath with mild exertion						
6. Frequent urge to eat						
7. Excessive snoring						
8. Drowsiness during the day						
9. Frequent mood swings						

TOTAL:
Resting pulse rate:
(Normal is 60 to 90)

Instructions: Check your milestones on the seventh day of each week. Put a check after each symptom that's still present. Then add the total number. By the third week, several of your symptoms should be gone and you'll be feeling much better.

The Stuffer's pulse is often above 85 beats per minute. Monitor your pulse weekly as it slows down to a more healthy rate.

At the end of six weeks, most people will have lost all or nearly all of their symptoms. If your symptoms of high metabolic rate have disappeared, and your pulse rate is normal, you are ready to move on to the next phase of your program.

If you have not lost weight, are still experiencing symptoms of a high metabolic rate, and continue to have frequent urges to eat, you may need to seek a structured form of help, such as group therapy or individual psychological counseling. Your need for this does not mean that you are weak or that you have failed. Individuals have different needs when it comes to weight loss. Decide to take the necessary steps to find the help that is right for you.

You should also go back and review the rules outlined for your diet. Any break with the rules might be responsible for your condition. For example, snacking between meals will increase, not satisfy, your hunger.

THE NEXT PHASE

Once your metabolic rate has been restored to a normal point, you can move on to the next phase of your diet. During this phase:

1. You will increase your calorie intake to a level that will allow you to lose weight over the long term. (Don't cheat by staying on your six-week allowance. If you maintain a level that is too low, you will become a Starver and stop losing.) To calculate your new calorie allowance, return to the equation near the front of this chapter. Eliminate step 7. Your new calorie allotment is the result of step 6, rounded off. (For example, in the sample used for women, the new allowance is 1456, rounded off to 1500 calories.)

2. You will be able to calculate your projected rate of weight loss. Once your metabolic rate is normal, your weight loss will occur in a more predictable way. You can calculate approximately how much you can expect to lose during a six-week period (not counting the additional benefits of your exercise program) by using this equation:

   a) Divide your daily calories by 3   ____

   b) Multiply the result × 42
        (the number of days in 6 weeks)   ____

   c) Divide the result by 3500
        (the number of calories per pound of fat) ____

Sample

Daily Calories: 1500

1500 divided by 3	=	500
500 × 42	=	21,000
21,000 divided by 3500	=	6*

*pound loss from eating, not including exercise

An Important Note to Stuffers

If you have a great deal of weight to lose, don't be discouraged by the amount of time it will take. Focus on your longer term life goals, and remember: This time the weight will *stay* off. This time you are losing not only pounds, but losing all of the attitudes and behaviors that made it so easy to regain weight when you lost it in the past. And this time, you will be doing it in a way that will not set up rebound weight gain.

Another thing: How often in the past have you used food as something different from its true intention? Have you used it for comfort? Entertainment? Love? Food will not replace love or help you find satisfaction. Begin to satisfy your needs with the things that will really work, not the false solutions.

NINE

Callaway Diet Food Plans

A week after Susan had started the program, she came into my office feeling a little disoriented.

"Dr. Callaway," she said, "I'm having a real psychological problem eating this much food. I was all set to go on a diet, but this doesn't feel like a diet. To tell you the truth, it kind of scares me."

Susan's reaction is a common one in the early stages of the program. Dieting has always meant deprivation, and most people have a hard time adjusting to getting full when they eat. And to add to their own fears, they have to contend with family and friends, who are always ready to jump in and tell them, "You're eating so *much*. Are you sure you're not just kidding yourself that you're dieting?"

I once had as a patient the mother superior of a religious order. She had a real problem to contend with. In her order, going without food or eating small amounts of food was considered a positive thing to do. But her metabolic rate was 25 percent below normal and she was cold, tired, and bloated. She had to eat more food in order to get her metabolic rate back up to normal. I put her on a diet of 1,600 calories a day, but when she returned to see me two weeks later, her metabolic rate was at the same level. "I couldn't eat that much," she said, nearly in tears. "All the sisters in the dining room were looking at me like I was overindulgent. I always had much more food on my plate than anyone else." I knew that if she was going to feel ashamed, the diet would never work in the long run—that's just human nature. I made this suggestion: "Can you make a special arrangement to eat apart from the group, just until your metabolic rate returns to normal? Your health depends on eating more." She agreed to try, and arranged to have meals in her quarters—doctor's orders. Away from the judgmental eyes of the other sisters, she was able to relax and eat the right amount. By the time she had reestablished a normal metabolic rate two months later, she felt so full of energy and so *healthy*, for the first time in years, that she instructed the kitchen to begin preparing larger portions for everyone in the convent.

Many of my patients take some ribbing from their friends when they start increasing their food intake. "What kind of diet doctor is this?" they laugh. It's hard to withstand the pressure of others—not to mention your own years of conditioning. The hardest period is the first three weeks, before you really start feeling better. It becomes easier once you see how much energy you have and how much better you look and feel.

To make the first three weeks easier, I asked nutritionist, Kristine Mehring, to help prepare menus that are full of delicious and varied selections. Kristine understands the way people really eat. Many diets fail in the long-term because they are boring and ignore the realities of American eating habits. These menus won't bore you into a catatonic state. There are ethnic dishes, wonderful casseroles, home baked goods, and even milkshakes. Kristine has used the menus and recipes with my patients, and they love being permitted so many of the foods they really enjoy.

How to Use the Menus

Each day's menu includes breakfast, lunch, and dinner food plans for four daily diet levels: 1,400 calories, 1,600 calories, 1,800 calories, and 2,000 calories. These are the most common average calorie allowances the people in our practice have used. Recipes are provided for the dishes that have an asterisk (*) next to them.

Don't drive yourself crazy calculating your meals down to the last calorie, but *do* stay within 50 calories of your allotment. In the beginning, measure your foods carefully until you are familiar with the amounts. Your primary focus in the early weeks should be twofold: one, to eat enough food; and two, to learn autonomy in creating your own meal plans so that you can join the "real world" of eating. Autonomy is important to success. Many diets fail because they are too rigid and ignore the typical ways that Americans eat. For example, according to the National Restaurant Association, more than 66 million Americans consume at least one meal outside the home every day. We want you to get comfortable enough with food that you won't have to stay out of restaurants or avoid the things you enjoy. We have also taken into account that over 60 percent of all women now work outside the home; the lunch menus are suitable for brown bagging.

At the end of this chapter is a blank Daily Meal Record. You may want to make copies of this form and use it to create your own meal plans.

Rules for Eating

Do not deviate from the following rules:

1. Eat three regularly scheduled meals per day and no snacks. You are not allowed to have snacks between meals, and you shouldn't be hungry. If you do get hungry, drink a cup of hot decaffeinated tea; you'll find that it satisfies you.

2. It is absolutely crucial that you do not skip any meals—this is what sets off binging. If you think you're going to have a harried, on-the-go day, carry your lunch and eat it in your car.

3. Your meals should be balanced throughout the day. About 25 percent of your calories should be consumed at breakfast, 30–35 percent at lunch, and the remainder at dinner. Get away from your old habit of "saving" calories. It will only encourage night binging.

4. No alcohol is allowed during the first six weeks. Alcohol is known to trigger binging. It also contains "empty" calories—that is, calories that have no nutritional value. You need all your calories as nutrients.

5. You may have up to two cups of caffeinated coffee or tea per day, and as much decaffeinated coffee or tea as you like. Too much caffeine falsely raises your metabolic rate. Get in the habit of drinking coffee and tea without sugar, including artificial sweeteners. Sugar can set off binging, and artificial sweeteners have the same effect. Replace diet sodas with mineral water or unsweetened seltzer.

Menus for 21 Days

Key to Terms:

t.	= teaspoon	sl.	= slice
T.	= tablespoon	oz.	= ounce
c.	= cup	*	= recipe provided

	1400 CAL.	1600 CAL.	1800 CAL.	2000 CAL.
Day 1				
BREAKFAST				
*Banana, Blueberry Bran Muffin (p. 143)	1	2	2	2
orange juice	½ c.	½ c.	½ c.	1 c.
wheat-flake cereal	1½ c.	¾ c.	1½ c.	1½ c.
skim milk	½ c.	½ c.	½ c.	½ c.

	1400 CAL.	1600 CAL.	1800 CAL.	2000 CAL.

LUNCH
Turkey Sandwich:

	1400 CAL.	1600 CAL.	1800 CAL.	2000 CAL.
bread	2 sl.	2 sl.	2 sl.	2 sl.
turkey	2 oz.	3 oz.	3 oz.	3 oz.
light mayonnaise	1 T.	1 T.	1 T.	1 T.
lettuce, tomato	As desired ————————			
apple	1 med.	1 med.	1 med.	1 lge.
*Cheesy Pita Chips (p. 144)	4	8	8	12

DINNER
Spaghetti Marinara:

	1400 CAL.	1600 CAL.	1800 CAL.	2000 CAL.
pasta	1½ c.	2 c.	2 c.	2½ c.
sauce	½ c.	½ c.	1 c.	1 c.
broccoli	1 c.	1 c.	1 c.	1 c.
French bread	1 sl.	1 sl.	2 sl.	2 sl.
grated Parmesan cheese	2 T.	2 T.	2 T.	2 T.
margarine	2 t.	2 t.	1 t.	1 t.

Day 2

BREAKFAST

	1400 CAL.	1600 CAL.	1800 CAL.	2000 CAL.
wheat-flake cereal	1½ c.	1½ c.	2¼ c.	2¼ c.
skim milk	1 c.	1 c.	1 c.	1 c.
banana	½ med.	1 med.	1 med.	1 med.
apple juice	0	0	0	½ c.

LUNCH
Salad Bar:

	1400 CAL.	1600 CAL.	1800 CAL.	2000 CAL.
chopped turkey or tuna	2 T.	2 T.	2 T.	3 T.
shredded cheese	2 T.	2 T.	2 T.	2 T.
croutons	½ c.	½ c.	½ c.	½ c.
garbanzo beans	½ c.	½ c.	½ c.	½ c.
lettuce and vegetables	As desired ————————			

	1400 CAL.	1600 CAL.	1800 CAL.	2000 CAL.
wheat roll	0	1 lge.	1 lge.	1 lge.
*Flavored Vinaigrette (p. 145)	1 T.	2 T.	2 T.	2 T.
mixed fruit	½ c.	½ c.	1 c.	1 c.

DINNER
*Grilled Citrus Chicken

	1400 CAL.	1600 CAL.	1800 CAL.	2000 CAL.
(p. 145)	3 oz.	3 oz.	4 oz.	4 oz.
sautéed zucchini	1 c.	1 c.	1 c.	1 c.
garlic, onion	As desired for flavor			
baked potato	1 med.	1 lge.	1 lge.	1 lge.
margarine	1 t.	2 t.	2 t.	3 t.

Day 3

BREAKFAST
wholegrain waffles

	1400 CAL.	1600 CAL.	1800 CAL.	2000 CAL.
(4½″ square)	2	3	3	3
margarine	2 t.	2 t.	2 t.	2 t.
light syrup	2 T.	2 T.	2 T.	2 T.
grapefruit	½	½	1	1

LUNCH
Triple Decker Sandwich:

	1400 CAL.	1600 CAL.	1800 CAL.	2000 CAL.
whole-wheat bread	3 sl.	3 sl.	3 sl.	3 sl.
cheese	1 oz.	1 oz.	1 oz.	1 oz.
turkey	0	1 oz.	1 oz.	1 oz.
ham	1 oz.	1 oz.	1 oz.	1 oz.
lettuce, tomato, onion	As desired			
light mayonnaise	1 T.	2 T.	2 T.	2 T.
orange	1 sm.	1 med.	1 lge.	1 lge.
oatmeal cookie	0	1 sm.	1 sm.	1 sm.

DINNER
*Marinated Flank Steak
with Dijon Sauce

	1400 CAL.	1600 CAL.	1800 CAL.	2000 CAL.
(p. 146)	3 oz.	3 oz.	3 oz.	3 oz.

	1400 CAL.	1600 CAL.	1800 CAL.	2000 CAL.
corn on the cob	1 ear	1 ear	2 ears	2 ears
margarine	1 t.	2 t.	2 t.	2 t.
salad greens	1 c.	1 c.	1½ c.	1 c.
*Flavored Vinaigrette (p. 145)	1 T.	1 T.	1 T.	1 T.
croutons	½ c.	½ c.	½ c.	½ c.
plain roll	0	0	1	2

Day 4

BREAKFAST

	1400 CAL.	1600 CAL.	1800 CAL.	2000 CAL.
bagel	1 med. (3 oz.)	1 lge. (4 oz.)	1 lge. (4 oz.)	1 lge. (4 oz.)
cream cheese	1 T.	1 T.	2 T.	2 T.
jam/jelly	0	0	0	1 T.
apple juice	4 oz.	4 oz.	8 oz.	8 oz.

LUNCH

Taco Salad:	1400 CAL.	1600 CAL.	1800 CAL.	2000 CAL.
lettuce, tomato	2 c.	2 c.	2 c.	2 c.
pinto beans	1 c.	1 c.	1 c.	1 c.
grated cheese	2 T.	4 T.	3 T.	4 T.
dressing	1 T.	2 T.	2 T.	2 T.
*Homemade Taco Chips (p. 147)	8	8	12	12

DINNER

	1400 CAL.	1600 CAL.	1800 CAL.	2000 CAL.
grilled salmon	3 oz.	3 oz.	4 oz.	4 oz.
*Mandarin Spinach Salad (p. 147)	1 c.	1 c.	1 c.	1 c.
*Lemon Rice (p. 148)	1 c.	1⅓ c.	1⅓ c.	1⅔ c.

Day 5

BREAKFAST

	1400 CAL.	1600 CAL.	1800 CAL.	2000 CAL.
whole-grain English muffin	1	1	1	1

	1400 CAL.	1600 CAL.	1800 CAL.	2000 CAL.
margarine	1 t.	1 t.	2 t.	2 t.
bran cereal with raisins	⅓ c.	⅔ c.	1 c.	1 c.
skim milk	½ c.	½ c.	½ c.	½ c.

LUNCH
Oriental Chicken Salad:

	1400 CAL.	1600 CAL.	1800 CAL.	2000 CAL.
chicken	2 oz.	2 oz.	2 oz.	2 oz.
rice	⅔ c.	⅔ c.	1 c.	1⅓ c.
chopped onion, celery	As desired			
*Oriental Chicken Salad Dressing (p. 148)	1 T.	2 T.	2 T.	2 T.
cooked vegetables (broccoli, spinach, green beans, squash, etc.)	½ c.	½ c.	½ c.	½ c.
wheat crackers	0	4	4	4
apple	0	1 med.	1 med.	1 lge.

DINNER

	1400 CAL.	1600 CAL.	1800 CAL.	2000 CAL.
*Hot Chili Chicken (p. 149)	3 oz.	3 oz.	3 oz.	3½ oz.
green peas	⅓ c.	⅔ c.	⅔ c.	⅔ c.
sliced carrots	½ c.	½ c.	½ c.	½ c.
baked potato	1 med.	1 med.	1 med.	1 lge.
frozen yogurt	0	4 oz.	4 oz.	4 oz.
margarine	1	0	2 t.	2 t.

Day 6

BREAKFAST

	1400 CAL.	1600 CAL.	1800 CAL.	2000 CAL.
whole-grain toast	2 sl.	2 sl.	2 sl.	2 sl.
peanut butter	1 T.	1 T.	1 T.	1 T.
cranberry juice	½ c.	½ c.	½ c.	1 c.
flavored, nonfat yogurt	0	½ c.	½ c.	½ c.

	1400 CAL.	1600 CAL.	1800 CAL.	2000 CAL.
LUNCH				
Ham Sandwich:				
whole-wheat bread	2 sl.	2 sl.	2 sl.	2 sl.
ham	2 oz.	2 oz.	2 oz.	2 oz.
mayonnaise	1 t.	1 t.	1 t.	2 t.
lettuce, tomato, mustard	As desired ———————			
vegetable soup	1 c.	1 c.	1 c.	1 c.
saltines	0	6	6	6
banana	½	½	½	1
DINNER				
lasagna (3″ × 4″ squares)	1	1½	1½	1½
sourdough roll	1 med.	1 med.	1 med.	1 med.
margarine	1 t.	1 t.	1½ t.	2 t.
green salad	1 c.	1 c.	1 c.	1 c.
*Flavored Vinaigrette (p. 145)	1 T.	1 T.	1 T.	1 T.

Day 7

	1400 CAL.	1600 CAL.	1800 CAL.	2000 CAL.
BREAKFAST				
whole-grain cereal	¾ c.	1 c.	1½ c.	1½ c.
skim milk	½ c.	½ c.	½ c.	1 c.
*Banana, Blueberry Bran Muffin (p. 143)	1	1	1	1
margarine	1 t.	1 t.	1 t.	1 t.
cranberry juice	½ c.	1 c.	1 c.	1 c.
LUNCH				
Pasta Salad:				
pasta	1 c.	1½ c.	1½ c.	2 c.
chopped, raw vegetables	½ c.	½ c.	½ c.	½ c.
shredded low-fat cheese	1 oz.	1 oz.	2 oz.	2 oz.

	1400 CAL.	1600 CAL.	1800 CAL.	2000 CAL.
*Pasta Salad Dressing (p. 149)	1 T.	2 T.	2 T.	3 T.
pita chips	4	4	8	8
cookie	1 med.	1 med.	1 med.	1 med.
DINNER				
*Chili Con Carne (p. 150)	1 c.	1 c.	1 c.	1½ c.
baked potato	1 med.	1 lge.	1 lge.	1 lge.
margarine	1 t.	1 t.	2 t.	2 t.
green salad	1 c.	1 c.	1 c.	1 c.
*Flavored Vinaigrette (p. 145)	1 T.	1 T.	1 T.	1 T.

Day 8

BREAKFAST

oatmeal sprinkled with 1 t. cinnamon and sugar	1 c.	1 c.	1 c.	1½ c.
skim milk	½ c.	1 c.	1 c.	1 c.
apple juice	½ c.	½ c.	1 c.	1 c.
margarine	1 t.	1 t.	1 t.	1 t.

LUNCH

*Chili Con Carne (p. 150) (leftovers)	1 c.	1 c.	1 c.	1 c.
grated low-fat cheese	0	0	2 T.	2 T.
saltines	6	6	6	12
orange	1 med.	1 med.	1 lge.	1 lge.
graham cracker squares	0	3	3	3

DINNER

*Chinese Grilled Pork (p. 150)	3 oz.	3 oz.	3 oz.	3 oz.
*Stir-fry Vegetable Medley (p. 151)	1 c.	1½ c.	1½ c.	1½ c.

	1400 CAL.	1600 CAL.	1800 CAL.	2000 CAL.
sliced steamed new potatoes	1½ c.	1½ c.	1½ c.	1½ c.
wheat roll	0	1 sm.	1 sm.	2 sm.
margarine	2 t.	2 t.	2 t.	2 t.

Day 9

BREAKFAST
waffles (4½" square)	2	2	3	3
margarine	1 t.	1 t.	2 t.	2 t.
sliced banana	½	1	1	1
skim milk	1 c.	1 c.	1 c.	1 c.

LUNCH
Stuffed Baked Potato:
potato	9 oz.	9 oz.	9 oz.	9 oz.
low-fat cheese	1 oz.	2 oz.	2 oz.	2 oz.
broccoli	½ c.	1 c.	1 c.	1 c.
margarine	1 t.	1 t.	1 t.	1 t.
apple	1 med.	1 med.	1 lge.	1 lge.
wheat crackers	0	0	0	4

DINNER
Spaghetti with Meat Sauce
cooked spaghetti	1 c.	1 c.	1½ c.	2 c.
sauce	1 c.	1 c.	1 c.	1 c.
Italian bread	1 sl.	2 sl.	2 sl.	2 sl.
garlic margarine	1 t.	1 t.	1 t.	1 t.
mixed green salad	1 c.	1 c.	1 c.	1 c.
*Flavored Vinaigrette (p. 145)	1 T.	1 T.	1 T.	1 T.
applesauce	½ c.	½ c.	½ c.	½ c.

	1400 CAL.	1600 CAL.	1800 CAL.	2000 CAL.
Day 10				
BREAKFAST				
bagel	1 med.	1 lge.	1 lge.	1 lge.
cream cheese	1 T.	1 T.	1½ T.	1½ T.
orange juice	4 oz.	4 oz.	4 oz.	8 oz.
LUNCH				
chicken noodle soup	1 c.	2 c.	2 c.	2 c.
Swiss Cheese on Rye:				
bread	2 sl.	2 sl.	2 sl.	2 sl.
low-fat Swiss cheese	2 oz.	2 oz.	2 oz.	2 oz.
lettuce, tomato, mustard	As desired ————			
light mayonnaise	1 T.	1 T.	2 T.	2 T.
pear	1	1	1	2
DINNER				
*Garden Burritos (p. 152)				
filling	1 c.	1½ c.	2 c.	2 c.
low-fat cheese	1 oz.	1½ oz.	2 oz.	2 oz.
pinto beans	⅓ c.	⅓ c.	⅓ c.	⅓ c.
sauce	½ c.	½ c.	½ c.	1 c.
flour tortillas	2	2	3	3
mixed fruit salad	1 c.	1 c.	1 c.	1 c.
Day 11				
BREAKFAST				
*Banana, Blueberry Bran Muffin (p. 143)	1	1	2	2
jam	1 T.	1 T.	1 T.	1 T.
*Fruit Smoothie (p. 153)	1 c.	1 c.	1½ c.	1½ c.
skim milk	½ c.	1 c.	½ c.	½ c.

	1400 CAL.	1600 CAL.	1800 CAL.	2000 CAL.
LUNCH				
Tuna or Chicken Salad:				
tuna or chicken (water-packed)	½ c.	½ c.	½ c.	¾ c.
light mayonnaise	1 T.	1 T.	1 T.	1 T.
chopped celery				
diced onion				
½ sliced tomato				
*Cheesy Pita Chips (p. 144)	8	8	12	12
grapes	1 c.	1 c.	1 c.	1 c.
whole-grain roll	0	1 sm.	1 sm.	1 sm.
DINNER				
lean roast beef	3 oz.	3 oz.	3 oz.	4 oz.
*Horseradish Sauce (p. 153)	2 T.	2 T.	2 T.	2 T.
green beans	1 c.	1 c.	1 c.	1 c.
*Mushroom Risotto (p. 154)	1 c.	1½ c.	2 c.	2 c.
ice milk	½ c.	½ c.	½ c.	½ c.

Day 12

	1400 CAL.	1600 CAL.	1800 CAL.	2000 CAL.
BREAKFAST				
scrambled egg	1	1	1	1
whole-wheat toast	2 sl.	2 sl.	2 sl.	2 sl.
margarine	1 t.	2 t.	2 t.	2 t.
jelly	0	0	1 T.	1 T.
grapefruit	½	½	½	1
LUNCH				
Pocket Sandwich:				
pita bread	1 lge.	1 lge.	1 lge.	1 lge.
roast beef (leftovers)	2 oz.	2 oz.	2 oz.	3 oz.
tomatoes, lettuce	As desired ———————			

	1400 CAL.	1600 CAL.	1800 CAL.	2000 CAL.
low-fat ranch dressing	2 T.	2 T.	2 T.	2 T.
orange	1 sm.	1 sm.	1 med.	1 med.
graham cracker squares	3	6	6	6

DINNER
Tostadas:

	1400	1600	1800	2000
tortilla shells (flour/corn)	2	2	2	2
shredded chicken	2 oz.	2 oz.	2 oz.	2 oz.
low-fat cheese	1 oz.	1 oz.	1½ oz.	2 oz.
tomato, lettuce	As desired			
sour cream	2 T.	2 T.	2 T.	2 T.
*Homemade Taco Chips (p. 147)	0	4	8	8
mixed fruit salad	½ c.	½ c.	½ c.	1 c.

Day 13

BREAKFAST

	1400	1600	1800	2000
English muffin	½	½	½	½
margarine	1 t.	1 t.	2 t.	2 t.
whole-grain-flake cereal	1½ c.	1½ c.	1½ c.	1½ c.
banana	½	1	1	1
skim milk	½ c.	½ c.	½ c.	1 c.

LUNCH
Pasta Salad:

	1400	1600	1800	2000
pasta	1 c.	1½ c.	1½ c.	1½ c.
sliced turkey or ham	1 oz.	1 oz.	1½ oz.	1½ oz.
part-skim mozzarella	1 oz.	1 oz.	1 oz.	1 oz.
chopped, raw vegetables	1 c.	1 c.	1 c.	1 c.
*Flavored Vinaigrette (p. 145)	1 T.	1 T.	2 T.	2 T.
wheat roll	1 sm.	1 sm.	1 sm.	2 sm.

	1400 CAL.	1600 CAL.	1800 CAL.	2000 CAL.
DINNER				
*Grilled Citrus Chicken (p. 145)	3 oz.	3 oz.	3 oz.	4 oz.
almond peas (+1 T. almonds)	½ c.	½ c.	½ c.	½ c.
brown rice	⅔ c.	1 c.	1 c.	1 c.
grapefruit/orange sections	½ c.	1 c.	1 c.	1 c.
tossed salad	0	0	1 c.	1 c.
*Flavored Vinaigrette (p. 145)	0	0	1 T.	1 T.

Day 14

	1400 CAL.	1600 CAL.	1800 CAL.	2000 CAL.
BREAKFAST				
whole-grain waffles, 5″ each	2	3	3	3
margarine	1 t.	1 t.	2 t.	2 t.
sliced banana, sprinkled with cinnamon/ sugar	1	1	1	1
orange juice	0	0	0	½ c.
LUNCH				
*Citrus Chicken Sandwich (p. 145) (leftovers)				
chicken	3 oz.	3 oz.	3 oz.	3 oz.
bun	1	1	1	1
lettuce, tomato	As desired ————————			
*Tarragon Mayonnaise (p. 155)	1 T.	1 T.	1 T.	1 T.
*Cheesy Pita Chips (p. 144)	4	4	8	12
apple	1 sm.	1 med.	1 med.	1 med.

	1400 CAL.	1600 CAL.	1800 CAL.	2000 CAL.
DINNER				
*Whole-Wheat Cheese and Vegetable Pizza (medium) (p. 155)	2 sl.	2 sl.	2½ sl.	2½ sl.
mixed green salad	1 c.	1 c.	1 c.	1 c.
*Flavored Vinaigrette (p. 145)	1 T.	1 T.	1 T.	1 T.
croutons	0	¼ c.	0	½ c.

Day 15

BREAKFAST				
whole-wheat toast	2 sl.	2 sl.	2 sl.	2 sl.
peanut butter	2 t.	2 t.	1 T.	1 T.
flavored low-fat yogurt	½ c.	½ c.	½ c.	1 c.
apple juice	½ c.	1 c.	1 c.	1 c.

LUNCH				
Turkey Sub Sandwich:				
sub roll (4 oz.)	1	1	1	1
sliced turkey	2 oz.	2 oz.	3 oz.	3 oz.
mayonnaise	1 t.	1 t.	1 t.	2 t.
lettuce, tomato	As desired —————————————————————
vegetable soup	0	1 c.	1 c.	1 c.
saltines	0	0	0	6

DINNER				
*Pork Dijonaise (p. 156)	3 oz.	3 oz.	3 oz.	3 oz.
new potatoes	1 c.	1½ c.	1½ c.	1½ c.
green beans	½ c.	½ c.	½ c.	1 c.
applesauce	½ c.	½ c.	1 c.	1 c.
wheat roll	0	1	1	1
margarine	0	0	0	1 t.

	1400 CAL.	1600 CAL.	1800 CAL.	2000 CAL.

Day 16

BREAKFAST

bagel	1 sm.	1 med.	1 med.	1 med.
cream cheese	1 T.	1 T.	1 T.	2 T.
*Berry Milkshake (p. 157)	1 c.	1 c.	1½ c.	1½ c.

LUNCH

baked potato	1 med.	1 med.	1 med.	1 lge.
margarine	1 t.	2 t.	2 t.	2 t.
vegetable soup	2 c.	2 c.	2 c.	2 c.
wheat crackers	0	0	6	6
fruit salad	½ c.	1 c.	1 c.	1 c.

DINNER

*Chicken, Cheese Enchiladas (p. 157)	2	2	2	2
*Mexican Rice (p. 158)	⅓ c.	⅔ c.	⅔ c.	1 c.
fruit ice/sorbet	0	0	⅓ c.	⅓ c.

Day 17

BREAKFAST

English muffin	1	1½	1½	1½
margarine	1 t.	1 t.	2 t.	2 t.
apple butter	1 T.	1 T.	1 T.	2 T.
flavored low-fat yogurt (vanilla, coffee, etc.)	½ c.	½ c.	½ c.	½ c.

LUNCH

*Chicken Cheese Enchiladas (leftovers) (p. 157)	2	2	2	2
*Homemade Taco Chips (p. 147)	0	6	6	6
orange	0	0	1 sm.	1 med.

	1400 CAL.	1600 CAL.	1800 CAL.	2000 CAL.
DINNER				
*Marinated Grilled				
Swordfish (p. 159)	3 oz.	3 oz.	3 oz.	3 oz.
*Lemon Rice (p. 148)	⅔ c.	1 c.	1 c.	1⅓ c.
corn on the cob	1	1	1	1
steamed broccoli	1 c.	1 c.	1 c.	1 c.
margarine	1 t.	1 t.	2 t.	2 t.

Day 18

	1400 CAL.	1600 CAL.	1800 CAL.	2000 CAL.
BREAKFAST				
oatmeal	1 c.	1 c.	1 c.	1 c.
cinnamon-sugar	1 t.	1 t.	1 t.	2 t.
whole-wheat toast	1 sl.	1 sl.	1 sl.	1 sl.
margarine	0	1 t.	1 t.	2 t.
skim milk	½ c.	½ c.	½ c.	½ c.
cranberry juice	⅓ c.	⅓ c.	⅔ c.	⅔ c.
LUNCH				
low-fat cottage				
cheese	½ c.	½ c.	¾ c.	¾ c.
mixed fruit salad	1 c.	1 c.	1 c.	1 c.
wheat crackers	8	8	8	12
DINNER				
Hamburger:				
extra-lean ground				
beef	3 oz.	3 oz.	3 oz.	3 oz.
whole-grain				
hamburger roll	1	1	1	1
tomato, lettuce,				
mustard	As desired			
catsup or light				
mayonnaise	1 T.	1 T.	1 T.	1 T.
potato salad	½ c.	⅔ c.	½ c.	1 c.
oatmeal cookies	0	0	1 sm.	2 sm.

	1400 CAL.	1600 CAL.	1800 CAL.	2000 CAL.

Day 19

BREAKFAST
*Banana Nut Pancakes
   (5″ diameter)

	1400 CAL.	1600 CAL.	1800 CAL.	2000 CAL.
(p. 160)	3	3	3	3
margarine	1 t.	2 t.	2 t.	2 t.
syrup	1 T.	1 T.	2 T.	2 T.
apple juice	½ c.	½ c.	½ c.	1 c.

LUNCH
Turkey Sandwich on Rye:

	1400 CAL.	1600 CAL.	1800 CAL.	2000 CAL.
whole-wheat bread	2 sl.	2 sl.	2 sl.	2 sl.
sliced turkey	2 oz.	2 oz.	2 oz.	3 oz.
light mayonnaise	1 T.	1 T.	1 T.	1 T.
lettuce, tomato	As desired ———————————————————		
orange	1 sm.	1 sm.	1 med.	1 med.
*Homemade Taco Chips				
(p. 147)	4	8	8	8

DINNER

	1400 CAL.	1600 CAL.	1800 CAL.	2000 CAL.
*Pasta Pie (p. 161)	⅛ pie	⅙ pie	¼ pie	¼ pie
garlic bread	2 sl.	1 sl.	1 sl.	1 sl.
margarine	1 t.	1 t.	1 t.	2 t.
sliced tomatoes	As desired ———————————————————		
mixed fruit	½ c.	½ c.	½ c.	1 c.

Day 20

BREAKFAST
*Banana, Blueberry Bran

	1400 CAL.	1600 CAL.	1800 CAL.	2000 CAL.
Muffin (p. 143)	1	1	2	2
whole-grain-flake cereal	¾ c.	¾ c.	¾ c.	¾ c.
skim milk	1 c.	1 c.	1 c.	1 c.
orange juice	½ c.	1 c.	½ c.	1 c.

	1400 CAL.	1600 CAL.	1800 CAL.	2000 CAL.
LUNCH				
Pasta Salad:				
cooked pasta	1 c.	1½ c.	1½ c.	1½ c.
chopped, raw vegetables	1 c.	1 c.	1 c.	1 c.
low-fat mozzarella cheese	2 oz.	2 oz.	3 oz.	3 oz.
*Pasta Salad Dressing (p. 149)	1 T.	1 T.	2 T.	2 T.
wheat roll	1	1	1	2
DINNER				
*White Fish with Tarragon Cream Sauce (p. 162)	3 oz.	3 oz.	3 oz.	3 oz.
steamed broccoli	1 c.	1 c.	1 c.	1 c.
*Lemon Rice (p. 148)	1 c.	1⅓ c.	1⅓ c.	1⅓ c.
mixed greens	As desired ————			
croutons	½ c.	½ c.	½ c.	½ c.
*Flavored Vinaigrette (p. 145)	1 T.	1 T.	1 T.	1 T.
cantaloupe	0	0	¼	½

Day 21

	1400 CAL.	1600 CAL.	1800 CAL.	2000 CAL.
BREAKFAST				
whole-grain-flake cereal	¾ c.	¾ c.	1½ c.	1½ c.
skim milk	½ c.	½ c.	1 c.	1 c.
raisins	2 T.	2 T.	2 T.	2 T.
poached or scrambled egg	1	1	1	1
whole-wheat toast	1 sl.	1 sl.	1 sl.	1 sl.
margarine	1 t.	1 t.	1 t.	2 t.

	1400 CAL.	1600 CAL.	1800 CAL.	2000 CAL.
LUNCH				
*Chili Con Carne (p. 150)	1 c.	1 c.	1¼ c.	1½ c.
baked potato	1 med.	1 med.	1 med.	1 med.
light margarine	1 T.	1 T.	1 T.	1 T.
mixed green salad	1 c.	1 c.	1 c.	1 c.
*Flavored Vinaigrette (p. 145)	1 T.	1 T.	1 T.	1 T.
DINNER				
*Tomato Basil Linguini with Vegetables (p. 162)	1½ c.	2 c.	2½ c.	2½ c.
French bread	1 c.	1 c.	1 c.	1 c.
French bread	1 sl.	1 sl.	1 sl.	2 sl.
garlic margarine	1 t.	1½ t.	1 t.	1 t.
ice milk	0	0	½ c.	½ c.

Recipes

BANANA, BLUEBERRY BRAN MUFFIN

Yield: 36 muffins
Calories: 130 each

INGREDIENTS

3	cups 100% bran cereal
1	cup boiling water
2	cups buttermilk
½	cup safflower oil
¾	cup sugar
2	eggs or
½	cup egg substitute
2	ripe bananas, mashed
1½	cups all-purpose flour

1½   cups whole-wheat flour, preferably stone-ground
2½   teaspoons baking soda
1   cup frozen blueberries

PREPARATION
1.   Preheat oven to 400°.
2.   In medium bowl, soak cereal in boiling water. Set aside to cool. Stir in buttermilk.
3.   In large bowl, mix oil and sugar until well blended. Beat in eggs, then mix in the bran-buttermilk mixture. Add mashed bananas to mixture.
4.   Sift together the all-purpose and whole-wheat flours and baking soda. Add to the bran mixture, stirring just enough to combine them. Fold in frozen blueberries.
5.   Divide batter among 36 well-greased muffin cups, about 2½″ × 1¼″, filling each cup about two-thirds full.
6.   Bake for 15 to 18 minutes. Place muffins on a rack to cool.

CHEESY PITA CHIPS

Yield: 16 chips
Calories: 125 for 4 chips

INGREDIENTS
1   bag large pita bread
     liquid margarine
     Parmesan cheese

PREPARATION
1.   Preheat oven to 350°.
2.   Split pitas in half and brush lightly with liquid margarine.
3.   Sprinkle with Parmesan cheese.
4.   Cut each pita into quarters.
5.   Bake until crisp—about 15 minutes.

FLAVORED VINAIGRETTE

Yield: 1½ cups
Calories: 45 per tablespoon

INGREDIENTS

1	cup flavored vinegar (raspberry, garlic, balsamic, etc.)
½	cup vegetable oil
2	tablespoons nonfat plain yogurt
1	teaspoon ground black pepper
	herbs as desired

PREPARATION

Combine all ingredients. Shake well. Refrigerate.

GRILLED CITRUS CHICKEN

Yield: 6 ½-breast servings
Calories: 206 per serving

INGREDIENTS

6	chicken breast halves, skinless
½	teaspoon grated lemon rind
½	teaspoon dry mustard
½	teaspoon oregano
1	teaspoon Worcestershire sauce
½	cup lemon juice
½	cup vegetable oil
4	green onions, chopped

PREPARATION

1. Mix lemon rind, mustard, oregano, and Worcestershire sauce in small bowl.
2. Gradually add lemon juice, then oil, and pour over chicken in a large bowl.
3. Marinate in refrigerator for 2 hours.
4. Grill in the oven until done.

MARINATED FLANK STEAK
WITH DIJON SAUCE

Yield: 12 ounces
Calories: 165 per 3-ounce serving

INGREDIENTS
Marinade:

1	bottle red wine vinegar & oil salad dressing
3	tablespoons lemon juice
2	garlic cloves, minced
2	tablespoons Worcestershire sauce
2	teaspoons ground black pepper
1	pound flank steak

Sauce:

½	cup tarragon vinegar
1	large shallot bulb, minced
¼	cup Dijon mustard
¾	cup plain yogurt

PREPARATION
Marinate Steak:

1. Combine all marinade ingredients in 8″ square baking dish.
2. Place steak in mixture and turn to coat both sides.
3. Refrigerate for 3 to 4 hours, basting occasionally.
4. Remove steak from marinade and broil or grill.

Sauce:

1. Boil vinegar and minced shallots in saucepan until reduced by half. Remove from heat and cool until lukewarm.
2. Add Dijon mustard, yogurt, and sugar to vinegar mix and stir well.
3. Place on low heat until heated throughout. (Serve sauce hot or chilled.)

HOMEMADE TACO CHIPS

Yield: 48 chips
Calories: 80 for 4 chips

INGREDIENTS

12   corn tortillas
     no-stick cooking spray
     salt (optional)

PREPARATION

1. Preheat oven to 350°.
2. Cut tortillas into quarters.
3. Place tortillas in a single layer on a cookie sheet sprayed with no-stick cooking spray.
4. Bake until crisp—about 10 to 15 minutes.

MANDARIN SPINACH SALAD

Yield: 8 cups
Calories: Salad: 105. Dressing: 45 per tablespoon

INGREDIENTS

Salad:

2   bunches fresh spinach
1   cup sliced mushrooms
1   6 oz. can mandarin oranges

Dressing:

½   cup safflower oil
½   cup white wine vinegar
2   tablespoons catsup
2   tablespoons sugar
½   teaspoon ground ginger
1   teaspoon dry mustard

PREPARATION

1. Wash, dry, and tear spinach into bite-size pieces.
2. Combine remaining salad ingredients in large bowl and refrigerate.

3. Mix dressing ingredients with a wire whisk until blended. Refrigerate until well chilled.
4. Pour dressing over salad and mix thoroughly.

LEMON RICE

Yield: about 6 cups
Calories: 80 per ⅓ cup

INGREDIENTS

2	cups uncooked rice
4	cups boiling water or defatted chicken broth
½	cup lemon juice
2	tablespoons grated lemon rind
1	tablespoon margarine

PREPARATION

1. Preheat oven to 350°.
2. Combine all ingredients in a 2- to 3-quart casserole.
3. Bake for 25 to 30 minutes.

ORIENTAL CHICKEN SALAD DRESSING

Yield: about 2 cups
Calories: 45 per tablespoon

INGREDIENTS

1½	tablespoons dry mustard
2	tablespoons sugar
1	tablespoon grated lemon peel
½	cup lemon juice
¼	cup light soy sauce
½	cup vegetable oil
¼	teaspoon ground ginger

PREPARATION

Mix ingredients, shake well, and refrigerate.

HOT CHILI CHICKEN

Yield: 8 ½-breast servings
Calories: 200 per ½ breast (3 ounces)

INGREDIENTS
6	tablespoons Dijon mustard
¼	cup canned green chilies
4	tablespoons lime juice
½	teaspoon dried coriander
1	teaspoon ground cumin
¼	cup safflower oil
4	chicken breasts, skinless, boneless
	breadcrumbs

PREPARATION
1. Preheat oven to 350°.
2. Mix mustard, chilies, lime juice, coriander, and cumin in blender. While processing, dribble safflower oil into mixture until it reaches the consistency of mayonnaise.
3. Halve chicken breasts. Brush each with mustard mixture on both sides.
4. Roll each in breadcrumbs.
5. Place in casserole pan that has been sprayed with no-stick spray. Bake for 20 to 25 minutes.

PASTA SALAD DRESSING

Yield: about 1 cup
Calories: 25 per tablespoon

INGREDIENTS
½	cup low-fat mayonnaise
½	cup low-fat yogurt
1	garlic clove
1	teaspoon dried basil

1   teaspoon dried tarragon
      dash of dried dill weed
2   tablespoons Parmesan cheese (optional)

PREPARATION
Mix all ingredients well and refrigerate.

CHILI CON CARNE

Yield: about 5¼ cups
Calories: 251 per ¾ cup

INGREDIENTS
1   pound extra-lean ground beef or cubed round
      steak
½   cup chopped onion
1   16-ounce can kidney beans, drained
1   16-ounce can whole, peeled tomatoes, drained
1   cup tomato sauce
½   tablespoon chili powder
      dash of cayenne pepper (optional)

PREPARATION
1.   Brown beef in nonstick skillet and drain well. Add
      onions and continue to cook until onions are tender.
2.   Stir in remaining ingredients.
3.   Cover and simmer for 30 minutes, stirring occa-
      sionally.

CHINESE GRILLED PORK

Yield: 6 4-ounce servings
Calories: 220 per 4-ounce serving

INGREDIENTS
¼   cup soy sauce
¼   cup sherry
1   tablespoon dark brown sugar

¼   cup lemon juice
½   teaspoon ground black pepper
6   pork tenderloins, 4 ounces each

PREPARATION

1. Combine soy sauce, sherry, brown sugar, lemon juice, and pepper.
2. Pour over pork in a shallow dish and marinate for several hours or overnight.
3. Remove pork from marinade and grill or broil until thoroughly cooked—about 30 to 45 minutes.

STIR-FRY VEGETABLE MEDLEY

Yield: 6 to 8 servings
Calories: 50 per cup

INGREDIENTS

1   tablespoon cornstarch
2   tablespoons sherry
2   teaspoons low-salt soy sauce
1   teaspoon oil
     no-stick cooking spray
1   cup sliced carrots
1   pound mushrooms, quartered
1   garlic clove
1   cup broccoli florets
2   cups snow peas
½   cup sliced water chestnuts
⅔   cup water
½   teaspoon chicken-flavored bouillon granules

PREPARATION

1. Combine cornstarch, sherry, and soy sauce and set aside.
2. Heat oil in a large skillet or wok, coated with cooking spray, over medium heat until hot.

3.   Add carrots, mushrooms, and garlic.
4.   Sauté 3 minutes or until crisp-tender, stirring constantly.
5.   Push vegetables to the side of the skillet and add broccoli, snow peas, and water chestnuts. Cook 3 minutes or until crisp-tender, stirring constantly.
6.   Stir in cornstarch mixture, water, and bouillon.
7.   Bring to boil and cook 1 minute or until thickened, stirring constantly.

GARDEN BURRITOS

Yield: 6-8 burritos
Calories: 245 per burrito

INGREDIENTS

Filling:
7 to 8 new potatoes, cleaned and quartered
½   onion, sliced
2   cups broccoli florets
1   yellow squash, sliced and quartered
1   zucchini, sliced and quartered
1   cup mushrooms, quartered

Sauce:
1   16-ounce can whole, peeled tomatoes
1   4-ounce can green chilies, chopped
½   cup sour cream
1   cup low-fat grated cheese
6   large flour tortillas

PREPARATION

1.   Steam new potatoes and onions until *al dente*. Add broccoli and squashes and steam 3 to 4 minutes longer. Add mushrooms and steam 1 to 2 minutes longer.
2.   *Sauce:* Puree tomatoes briefly and pour into saucepan. Add green chilies and heat over low flame

for 20 minutes. Just before serving, stir in sour cream.

3. Assemble by placing vegetables on one side of flour tortillas, sprinkling each with 2 tablespoons grated cheese and small amount of sauce. Roll up, place on plates, and top with more sauce.

FRUIT SMOOTHIE

Yield: about 2 cups
Calories: 60 per ½ cup

INGREDIENTS
1   cup orange juice
½   banana
½   cup low-fat yogurt
     several ice cubes

PREPARATION
Place all ingredients in blender. Cover and blend until smooth.

HORSERADISH SAUCE

Yield: about ½ cup
Calories: 45 for 2 tablespoons

INGREDIENTS
1   tablespoon horseradish
¼   cup low-fat sour cream

PREPARATION
Combine thoroughly and refrigerate.

MUSHROOM RISOTTO

Yield: about 3 cups
Calories: 160 per cup

INGREDIENTS

2   cups fresh, sliced mushrooms
2   tablespoons minced shallots
1   tablespoon lemon juice
    vegetable cooking spray
1   cup Italian Arborio rice
2   cups hot water
1   teaspoon chicken-flavored bouillon granules
2   tablespoons grated Parmesan cheese
1   teaspoon pepper

PREPARATION

1. Combine mushrooms, shallots, and lemon juice in saucepan coated with cooking spray. Cover and cook over medium heat 5 minutes or until tender, stirring occasionally. Stir in rice and cook 3 more minutes, stirring occasionally.
2. Combine hot water and bouillon granules. Add ½ cup bouillon mixture to saucepan. Cook 2 to 3 minutes or until liquid is absorbed, stirring occasionally. Repeat procedure with remaining bouillon mixture, adding ½ cup at a time and making sure each portion is absorbed before adding the next.
3. Remove from heat. Stir in cheese and pepper. Spoon into serving bowls.

TARRAGON MAYONNAISE

Yield: ¼ cup
Calories: 45 per tablespoon

INGREDIENTS

¼ cup light mayonnaise
1 tablespoon tarragon vinegar
1 teaspoon dried tarragon

PREPARATION
Mix well and refrigerate.

WHOLE-WHEAT CHEESE AND VEGETABLE PIZZA

Yield: 1 pie (8 slices)
Calories: 265 per slice

INGREDIENTS

Crust:

1 cup whole-wheat flour
1 cup white flour
1 teaspoon baking powder
½ teaspoon baking soda
¾ cup water
2 tablespoons vegetable oil

Sauce:

2 tablespoons olive oil
½ cup minced onions
4 small garlic cloves, minced
3 pounds tomatoes, peeled, seeded, and coarsely chopped
2 tablespoons dried basil
2 teaspoons dried oregano
¼ teaspoon ground black pepper
salt as desired

Toppings:
assorted vegetables
2   cups shredded mozzarella cheese

PREPARATION

Crust:
1. Mix dry ingredients together, add water, and mix well— the consistency will be stiff.
2. Work in oil with hands until thoroughly combined.
3. Roll out to 10″ diameter and place in well-oiled pizza pan.

Sauce:
1. Heat oil over low flame. Add onions and cook until transparent.
2. Add garlic and tomatoes and cook until it reaches consistency of sauce.
3. Add herbs and simmer uncovered 10 to 15 minutes.

Cook:
1. Preheat oven to 350°.
2. Top crust with sauce, cheese, and vegetables.
3. Bake 20 to 25 minutes on lower rack, or until crust is brown and cheese bubbles slightly.

PORK DIJONAISE

Yield: 4 3-ounce servings
Calories: 165 per 3-ounce serving

INGREDIENTS
1   pound pork tenderloin, well trimmed
½   cup Dijon mustard
2   teaspoons dry mustard
1   tablespoon parsley flakes
1   teaspoon dried thyme
½   teaspoon ground black pepper

PREPARATION

1. Mix mustard and herbs and spread evenly on both sides of pork.
2. Grill pork until well done.

BERRY MILKSHAKE

Yield: 2½ cups
Calories: 120 per 1¼-cup serving

INGREDIENTS

½ banana, chopped in small pieces
1 cup skim milk
½ cup plain, nonfat yogurt
1 cup strawberries or raspberries, halved
2 teaspoons vanilla extract
1 to 2 teaspoons sugar (optional)
  ice cubes

PREPARATION
Place all ingredients in blender and process until smooth.

CHICKEN, CHEESE ENCHILADAS

Yield: 12 enchiladas
Calories: 235 each

INGREDIENTS

1 pound boneless, skinless chicken breasts, chopped into pieces approximately 2 inches in diameter
1 15-ounce can Hunt's Special Tomato Sauce
½ teaspoon dried coriander
½ teaspoon ground cumin
12 corn or flour tortillas
1 cup shredded cheddar cheese
1 cup shredded Monterey Jack cheese

Sauce:

2   tablespoons margarine
2   tablespoons all-purpose flour
2   cups skim milk
1   4-ounce can green chilies

PREPARATION

1. *Sauce:* Melt margarine in saucepan. Add flour and
    stir over medium heat. Whisk in milk and con-
    tinue to stir until sauce has thickened, then add
    chilies.
2. Preheat oven to 350°.
3. Place chicken and tomato sauce in medium sauce-
    pan and cook over medium heat until chicken has
    absorbed most of the sauce (approximately 20 min-
    utes). Add spices.
4. Steam tortillas between moistened towels in the
    microwave for 1 to 2 minutes to soften. On each
    tortilla, place 2 tablespoons of chicken mixture
    on one side and top with 1 tablespoon of each
    cheese.
5. Roll tortillas and place seam-side down in a 13″ × 9″
    pan. Dribble sauce over tortillas. Cover with foil
    and bake for 15 to 20 minutes.

MEXICAN RICE

Yield: about 3 cups
Calories: 80 per ½-cup serving

INGREDIENTS

1   cup uncooked brown rice
1   15-ounce can chicken broth, defatted
⅔   cup water
½   cup chopped green pepper
½   cup peeled, chopped tomatoes

PREPARATION

1. Preheat oven to 350°.
2. Mix all ingredients in a 2-quart casserole that has been coated with no-stick cooking spray. Cover.
3. Bake for 1 hour and 15 minutes, or until all liquid has been absorbed, stirring once halfway through cooking to distribute vegetables throughout the rice.

MARINATED GRILLED SWORDFISH

Yield: 6 steaks, 4 ounces each
Calories: 220 per 4-ounce serving

INGREDIENTS

6	swordfish steaks, approximately ½″ thick
½	cup light soy sauce
½	cup dry sherry
¼	cup lemon juice
2	tablespoons Worcestershire sauce
¼	cup vegetable oil
3	garlic cloves, minced
1	tablespoon Dijon mustard

PREPARATION

1. Combine all marinade ingredients and marinate swordfish steaks in refrigerator for no more than 2 to 3 hours.
2. Grill approximately 5 minutes on each side, until done, brushing with marinade.

BANANA NUT PANCAKES

Yield: 18 pancakes (5″ diameter)
Calories: 225 for 3 pancakes

INGREDIENTS

Dry:
2⁄3   cup whole-wheat flour
2⁄3   cup white flour
2   teaspoons sugar
1   teaspoon baking powder
1⁄4   teaspoon baking soda
1⁄2   teaspoon ground cinnamon

Liquid:
1   cup buttermilk
1⁄4   cup skim milk (may require slightly more)
2   eggs
1   tablespoon vegetable oil
1   teaspoon vanilla extract
2   ripe bananas, mashed
1⁄4   cup chopped pecans
      nonstick vegetable spray

PREPARATION
1.   Mix together all dry ingredients.
2.   In second bowl, beat liquid ingredients together, then add to dry ingredients. Stir to combine.
3.   Allow batter to stand for about 10 minutes.
4.   Heat griddle or large nonstick frying pan over medium heat. (Use nonstick spray as required.)
5.   Pour batter to make pancakes about 5″ diameter.
6.   Flip pancakes when bottoms are golden brown and tops begin to bubble.

PASTA PIE

Yield: 1 pie (8 slices)
Calories: 282 per slice

INGREDIENTS

1	8-ounce package vermicelli
¾	pound extra-lean ground beef
2	tablespoons liquid margarine
½	teaspoon minced garlic cloves
1	cup part-skim ricotta cheese
¼	cup grated Parmesan cheese
1	tablespoon chopped parsley
1	15-ounce can tomato sauce
1	6-ounce can tomato paste
¼	cup dry white wine
½	teaspoon dried basil
½	teaspoon dried oregano
1	cup shredded part-skim mozzarella cheese

PREPARATION

1. Cook pasta according to package directions, omitting salt.
2. Preheat oven to 350°.
3. Brown meat in nonstick skillet and drain grease.
4. Combine pasta, margarine, and garlic and press into pie pan.
5. Mix ricotta, Parmesan, and parsley and spread mixture over pasta shell.
6. Combine beef, tomato sauce, tomato paste, wine, basil, and oregano and simmer approximately 15 minutes.
7. Pour beef mixture on top of ricotta and pasta. Top with mozzarella cheese. Bake until heated through.
8. Cool slightly, cut pie into wedges, and top with shredded mozzarella cheese.

WHITEFISH WITH
TARRAGON CREAM SAUCE

Yield: 4 fillets, 4 ounces each
Calories: 204 per fillet

INGREDIENTS
4	whitefish fillets
½	cup light mayonnaise
½	cup Parmesan cheese, grated
2	tablespoons lemon juice
2	teaspoons dried tarragon

PREPARATION
1. Preheat oven to 350°.
2. Place whitefish in a shallow baking dish treated with nonstick spray.
3. Mix all other ingredients in a small bowl and spread 1 tablespoon on top of each fillet. Bake for about 15 minutes or until fish flakes when prodded with a fork.

TOMATO BASIL LINGUINI
WITH VEGETABLES

Yield: 8 1-cup servings of pasta. 8 1-cup servings of vegetables. 8 2-tablespoon servings of sauce
Calories: 275 per 1-cup serving of each with sauce

INGREDIENTS

Linguini Mix:
16	ounces uncooked linguini
¼	cup liquid margarine
¼	cup plain, nonfat yogurt
½	cup grated Parmesan cheese

Sauce:
2   garlic cloves
1   teaspoon safflower oil
1   can peeled, whole tomatoes
1   tablespoon dried basil
      salt and pepper to taste

Vegetables:
1   bunch broccoli, cut into florets
2   zucchini, sliced
2   winter squash, sliced
2   cups snow peas (or vegetables of your choosing)

PREPARATION
1.   Cook pasta according to package directions, then
      toss hot pasta with margarine, yogurt, and Parmesan
      cheese.
2.   Heat garlic in oil. Chop tomatoes and add to garlic-
      oil mixture. Heat thoroughly until tomatoes form
      a sauce. Add spices.
3.   Steam vegetables.
4.   Pour cooked pasta onto a large, heated platter.
      Make a well in the center and place vegetables
      there. Drizzle sauce over vegetables.

Nutrition Guide to Common Foods

Help for creating healthy meal plans. Planning well-
rounded, nutritional meals doesn't have to be dull. To
the contrary, once you understand the basics of good
eating and know how to calculate your calorie intake to
be sure you're eating enough, you'll enjoy a control
you've never had before.

How to use the food charts. The following charts list
recommended foods in nine categories: (1) fruits, (2)
vegetables, (3) grains/cereals/breads, (4) pasta/beans/rice/
noodles/nuts, (5) dairy, (6) poultry/fish, (7) beef/meat,

(8) oils/margarine, and (9) miscellaneous. The foods in each list have been selected with the following values in mind: low fat, low cholesterol, low sugar, and low salt. Numbers indicate the approximate percentage of protein, fat, or carbohydrate in each food.

When purchasing commercially packaged foods, check the nutritional information for sodium, fat, and cholesterol content. You may want to purchase one of the guides to the nutritional content of commercial foods, since many packages do not list all of the information.

NUTRITIONAL VALUES OF COMMON FOODS

Fruits

SERVING	CALORIES	%P	%F	%C
1 cup orange juice	110			100
1 medium apple	80	3		97
½ cantaloupe	80	9		91
10 seedless grapes	35			100
1 medium orange	90			100
1 peach	40	9		91
1 pear	100	4	8	88
1 cup sliced pineapple	80	5		95
1 plum	30			100
1 cup strawberries	55	6	14	80
1 cup blueberries	82	4	6	90
½ grapefruit	50	7		93
6 dried prunes	120	4	4	92
3 small apricots	55	7		93
½ cup unsweetened applesauce	53	2		98

Vegetables

SERVING	CALORIES	%P	%F	%C
1 cup cooked carrots	50	8		92
1 cup cooked collard greens	65	40	12	48

SERVING	CALORIES	%P	%F	%C
1 medium baked potato	145	11		89
1 cup cooked spinach	40	38	17	45
1 cup cooked summer squash	30	22		78
1 cup cooked winter squash	130	9	7	84
1 medium baked sweet potato	160	5	5	90
1 medium steamed artichoke	53	18	3	79
1 cup cooked asparagus	30	38		62
1 cup cooked green beans	30	33		67
1 cup cooked broccoli	40	42		58
1 cup cooked cauliflower	30	37		63
1 cup boiled eggplant	38	20		80
½ cup cooked green peas	67	8		92
1 cup chopped carrots	45	8		92
1 cup chopped celery	5			100
1 cup endive	10	33		67
2 cups romaine lettuce	20	33		67
1 cup sliced mushrooms	20	40		60
4 chopped radishes	5			100
1 cup raw spinach	15	50		50
1 medium sliced tomato	25	14		86

Grains/Cereals/Breads

SERVING	CALORIES	%P	%F	%C
1 slice cracked-wheat bread	65	14	12	74
1 slice whole-wheat bread	60	14	16	70
1 slice rye bread	65	13	12	75
1 medium bran muffin	110	10	36	54
1 English muffin	130	12	11	77
1 slice French bread	72	12	11	77
1 medium nut muffin	165	13	9	78
2 bread sticks	86	12	28	60
3 rye crackers	72	14	4	82
4 saltines	52	8	24	68
4 wheat crackers	64	7	29	64
1 ounce bran flakes	90	13	4	83
1 ounce shredded wheat	100	11	6	83

SERVING	CALORIES	%P	%F	%C
1 cup cooked farina	135	12	3	85
1 ounce corn flakes	110	7	2	91
1 cup cooked oatmeal	145	16	16	68

Pasta/Beans/Rice/Noodles/Nuts

SERVING	CALORIES	%P	%F	%C
1 cup cooked spaghetti w/tomato sauce	260	14	32	54
1 cup cooked long-grain brown rice	173	9	2	89
1 cup cooked macaroni	192	15	1	84
1 cup cooked egg noodles	200	15	5	80
1 cup cooked spaghetti	192	15	1	84
1 corn tortilla	32	10	11	79
1 cup cooked lentil beans	210	29		71
½ cup cooked lima beans	130	25	1	74
½ cup cooked navy beans	112	25	2	73
4 ounces bean curd (tofu)	82	39	48	13
1 ounce sunflower seeds	162	15	73	12

Dairy

SERVING	CALORIES	%P	%F	%C
4 ounces low fat (1%) cottage cheese	82	72	15	13
1 ounce part-skim mozzarella cheese	80	40	55	5
½ cup part-skim ricotta cheese	171	33	52	15
1 hard-boiled or poached egg	80	29	66	5
1 cup skim milk	85	40		60
1 cup low-fat fruit yogurt	230	16	15	69
1 cup nonfat plain yogurt	125	43		57
1 tablespoon grated Parmesan cheese	23	69	31	

Poultry/Fish

SERVING	CALORIES	%P	%F	%C
3 ounces skinless chicken, roasted, white meat	165	78	22	
3.5 ounces skinless turkey, roasted, white meat	135	98	2	
3.5 ounces water-packed tuna	127	98	2	
3 ounces steamed shrimp	102	84	8	8
3 ounces salmon, broiled/baked	149	57	43	
3 ounces perch fillet, broiled/baked	113	85	15	
3 ounces sea bass, broiled/baked	117	72	28	
3 ounces flounder, broiled/baked	101	69	31	
3 ounces scallops, broiled/baked	106	59	28	13

Beef/Meat

SERVING	CALORIES	%P	%F	%C
3 ounces broiled lean tenderloin beef	167	57	43	
3 ounces roasted lean round eye	155	65	35	
3 ounces broiled lean veal steak	123	68	32	
3 ounces ground lean beef	217	41	59	

Oils/Margarine

NOTE: Vegetable fats have no cholesterol, but avoid palm oil and coconut oil, since they're high in saturated fat.

SERVING	CALORIES	%P	%F	%C
1 tablespoon margarine (corn oil)	100		100	
1 tablespoon diet salad dressing	22		36	64
1 tablespoon olive oil	119		100	
1 tablespoon soybean oil	120		100	
1 tablespoon safflower oil	120		100	
1 tablespoon sesame oil	120		100	
1 tablespoon sunflower oil	120		100	
1 tablespoon corn oil	120		100	

Miscellaneous

SERVING	CALORIES	%P	%F	%C
1 tablespoon jam/preserves	14			100
1 tablespoon diet jam	2			100
1 tablespoon apple butter	33		3	97
1 tablespoon vinegar	2	trace	———	
1 tablespoon horseradish	2	trace	———	
1 tablespoon (prepared) mustard	15	trace	———	
1 tablespoon catsup	16	trace	———	
1 cup plain popped popcorn	31	8	8	84

DAILY FOOD RECORD

Week ____ Day _____ Date _____ Calories Allowed ____

FOOD OR BEVERAGE	CALORIES	TIME	LOCATION	COMMENTS

DAILY FOOD RECORD

Week _____ Day _____ Date _____ Calories Allowed _____

FOOD OR BEVERAGE	CALORIES	TIME	LOCATION	COMMENTS

TEN

The Exercise Bonus

Reduced activity is a major cause of obesity in America today. In our clinical studies, we have found that the only people who consistently lose large amounts of weight and maintain their loss for up to ten years are those who incorporate a regular program of exercise.

All three of our programs include a plan for moderate aerobic exercise, but not all three plans begin at once. Only the Stuffer can begin exercising right away. Both the Starver and the Skipper must wait until their metabolic rates are restored to normal. This is because exercise exacerbates the starvation defense, when the body is burning more than it is consuming. Here is what we have found regarding the effects of exercise, in combination with diet, on the metabolic rate:

- **Low-Calorie Diet + Exercise.** Your metabolic rate rises briefly while you're exercising, but shoots back down when you stop.

- **Adequate Diet + Occasional Exercise.** You burn more calories while you exercise and for a short while thereafter because your metabolic rate is maintained at a higher level for a longer period of time.

- **Adequate Diet + Sustained Aerobic Exercise (twenty to sixty minutes).** The best of all. If you exercise regularly, your metabolic rate stays up and you continue to burn calories for as long as ten to twelve hours at a higher rate.

Regular exercise appears to lessen the risk for a number of chronic health problems, including heart disease, adult-onset diabetes, and osteoporosis. The best form of exercise is a moderate program of low-impact aerobics. Aerobic exercise is sustained movement that elevates the heart rate and burns fat. It also increases the production of norepinephrine, which makes you feel more energetic and elevates your mood. The key to aerobics is to sustain the activity. Stop-and-start exercises (such as calisthenics) are not aerobic.

According to the American College of Sports Medicine, aerobic exercise has these major benefits for the dieter:

1. Exercise promotes loss of fat. Body-fat loss can be achieved through a regular exercise program, especially if it is aerobic. It is their recommendation that for body-fat loss, exercise should be done at least three times per week, with a goal of expending 900 calories in exercise over the course of a week.

2. Exercise improves cardiovascular fitness. Aerobic exercise three to five times a week, for periods of fifteen to sixty minutes, improves overall fitness and reduces the risk of heart disease.

3. Another advantage of exercise is that it helps to blunt food cravings and hunger. You can incorporate it into your day at those times when food is normally a problem (e.g., early evening for the Skipper).

In a report on the relative merits of various exercise approaches for weight reduction, Louis M. Sheldahl of the Veterans Administration Medical Center, an expert on exercise and its relationship to health and weight control, suggests the following:

Walking. Walking is highly rated as a form of aerobic exercise, especially for people who are overweight, since it places less stress on weight-bearing joints than jogging does. From a convenience standpoint, walking is well suited to the average American lifestyle in that it can be done anywhere, anytime, without special equipment or clothes, by oneself or with others. On the other hand, walking requires more time to get the same effects that are produced with higher-intensity activities like jogging.

Jogging. Jogging is not suggested for people who are overweight, since there is too much danger of injury to the joints. However, for those who are already at a healthy weight, it might be a preferred form of exercise, since it takes less time to achieve the same results as walking.

Bicycling. Biking has become one of the most popular forms of aerobic exercise in America today, as is evidenced by the increasing number of bicycle tours and competitive events available. There are even several magazines devoted specifically to this sport—such as *Bicycling* and *Cycling*. To gain the maximum aerobic benefits, bicycling must be done continuously over a period of twenty-five to thirty-five minutes. A leisurely ride, stopping and starting at traffic lights and corners, will not increase the heart rate sufficiently. Most cities have bike paths in parks or along waterfronts that allow bikers to enjoy uninterrupted riding.

Exercise bicycle. This form of exercise has advantages for the obese, since it involves little stress on the joints, the intensity can easily be adjusted, and it can be done indoors and in private. However, it involves an expense, and takes up room. There is also some degree of discomfort in sitting on a bicycle for an extended period of time, and it gets boring.

Aerobic dance. There have been a significant number of injuries reported in the knees and lower legs from aerobic dancing, which often involves jumping, running, and moving rapidly. It is not recommended for those who are very overweight, unless the program is of a low-impact variety. Some people prefer this kind of group setting, while others find it embarrassing, so that benefit is up to the individual. However, one problem with group exercise is that the pace is set at a level that allows little control by the individual. It's possible to lose many of the benefits by not performing the exercises correctly. Make sure you have a skilled instructor.

Swimming. For the obese, swimming or other water sports can be beneficial, since the buoyancy effect of water can reduce the weight-bearing stress on joints. In addition, the thermodynamic effect of water can reduce the tendency to overheat while exercising. However, swimming takes some skill to get the maximum aerobic benefits. Group water-aerobics programs might be good alternatives.

When you choose an exercise, it's important to select one that is tailored to your needs. Factors you should consider include:

1. *Convenience.* If it's not easily available and realistic to your schedule, you'll have a hard time maintaining the regularity of the program.

2. *Health and weight.* If you are very overweight, you need to avoid exercises that could damage your joints. You also may find it difficult to perform these exercises correctly, given your size. A further consideration is how comfortable you will feel in the exercise environment— in other words, whether you'll be self-conscious about exercising in a group environment such as an aerobics class or public swimming pool.

3. *Avoiding boredom.* The problem with many exercise regimens is that they're repetitious and boring. You should choose an activity that will give you some enjoyment so you won't dread doing it. Or choose two or three different forms of exercise and alternate them.

4. *Moderation.* Don't "go for the burn." Moderate, regular exercise, gradually increased over a period of time, is the best method.

Incorporating Exercise into Your Plan

When you begin your exercise plan (at the start for Stuffers, and later for Starvers and Skippers), begin slowly and gradually increase the duration and intensity of your exercise activity. Unless your doctor advises differently, follow the guidelines as they are stated below and measure your progress on the Activity Scale (p. 175).

Rule 1: Choose your activity from this list. You may stick with one or choose more than one and alternate:

Brisk walking	Water sports
Jogging	Bicycling machine
Jogging in place	Aerobic dance/exercise
Swimming	

Rule 2: Exercise every day to enhance aerobic effects and keep your metabolic rate up.

Rule 3: Exercise at the same hour every day.

Rule 4: Begin slowly and gradually increase the time. Fat-burning occurs with increased duration at moderate intensity.

Example:
Begin brisk walking, 10 minutes daily.
Increase to 15 minutes daily.
Increase to 20 minutes daily.
Add 1-pound hand weights while continuing at a moderate pace for 20 minutes daily.

Here is a rule of thumb for measuring intensity levels for brisk walking:

MEN:
Medium intensity   =   1 mile in 13½ minutes
Low intensity   =   1 mile in 16 minutes

WOMEN:
Medium intensity   =   1 mile in 14½ minutes
Low intensity   =   1 mile in 17 minutes.

Rule 5: Record your progress on the Activity Scale. Below is a sample for one week. For each day, record the exercise, the time of day, the duration, the intensity (speed), and the addition of hand weights.

ACTIVITY SCALE

	M	T	W	TH	F	S	S
Activity							
Level of Intensity							
Duration (minutes)							

ELEVEN

Cultural-Biological Harmony

Usually, people approach diets wearing blinders. We think of ourselves as "just bodies": good bodies, bad bodies, slim bodies, fat bodies, beautiful bodies, ugly bodies—and so on.

Yet, the very fact that we diet demonstrates that we are far more than the sum of our physical parts. Only humans *choose* to deprive themselves of food at the expense of health. And only humans are capable of becoming aware of and thinking about our bodies as they relate to our "total selves." For humans, biological realities always carry psychological implications.

The following six exercises are designed to bridge the gap between the way you are biologically and the way you think of yourself as a person. As I have said many times, it is not enough to have a goal for your body unless it is aligned with other goals in your life. If you have put things on hold until you lose weight, and believe that being thin will miraculously make you more successful, more desirable, and more fulfilled, you need to take another look at why you've been selling yourself so short.

There is one exercise for each of the first six weeks of the diet. Use your notebook to record your answers and reflections.

WEEK 1:
Where Did You Get Your Shape?

Your genetic inheritance binds your personal history to that of your ancestors. Although you are free to choose your style of dress and alter many aspects of your appearance (your hair color, the shape of your nose, etc.), your basic body shape and size are inherited.

At least one person in the last two generations of your family has a shape and size similar to yours. Have you ever stopped to consider who among your parents, grandparents, aunts, and uncles were the benefactors of your body? Have you observed (if you have sons, daughters, nieces, nephews, or grandchildren) who, if anyone, in the family has inherited *your* shape?

1. Consider members of your family and their body shapes. Find those members on the list below whose body shapes are similar to yours. (On your own, add other relatives as appropriate.) Put a check by those people.

Father	_____	Aunt (Father's side)	_____
Mother	_____	Uncle (Father's side)	_____
Grandfather (Mother's)	_____	Brother	_____
Grandmother (Mothers')	_____	Sister	_____
Aunt (Mother's side)	_____	Son	_____
Uncle (Mother's side)	_____	Daughter	_____
Grandfather (Father's)	_____	Niece	_____
Grandmother (Father's)	_____	Nephew	_____
		Grandchild	_____

2. List the people from whom you inherited your body.

_____

_____

3. List the people who have inherited your body.

_____

_____

4. Describe the inherited characteristics of your body.

_____

_____

5. Write a brief reflection about what you have learned from this exercise. Has it given you a greater appreciation of your body?

_____

_____

WEEK 2:
The Admiration Scale

Most people judge themselves more harshly than they judge others. You may associate your weight problem with a whole series of personal characteristics that diminish your worth in your own eyes. And yet, you wouldn't dream of using the same measure on those whom you love and admire. Try this exercise and see for yourself.

1. Write the names of two members of your family whom you love and admire the most.

_____

_____

2. Write the names of two friends whom you love and admire the most.

_____

_____

3. Write the names of two people, apart from family and friends (teachers, clergy, coaches, doctors, etc.), whom you admire and who have played an important role in your life.

_____

_____

4. Write the names of two people you do not know (public figures, historical figures, authors, artists, scientists, etc.) but for whom you have a great deal of admiration.

_____

_____

5. For each of the eight people, list three qualities that you appreciate the most about them.

Family   Friends   Influential People   Public Figures

_____

_____

6. Write how many times you mentioned aspects of physical appearance among the qualities you most appreciate.

_____

_____

7. Reflect on your answers. How important is the size, shape, and overall appearance of those whom you love and admire?

_____

_____

8. Answer this question: How important do you think your size and shape are to the people who love and admire you?

_____

_____

WEEK 3:
What Does Food Mean to You?

You have invested food with a great deal of meaning, and this is what has separated you from "normal" eaters. Maybe it's a conditioned response—you were taught

to think of food in a certain way. Many religions assign
symbolic meaning to food; some equate eating with
indulgence and fasting with virtue.

Or maybe your problems with food began the first
time you dieted to conform to a thin ideal. Whatever its
basis, you now have a preoccupation with food—either
consuming it or avoiding it. You want to rise above
your preoccupation.

What, for you, are the emotional implications of food?
Check all the responses that apply:

1. _____ When you were young, your parents used
food to reward you for good behavior.
2. _____ When you were young, you were deprived
of food as a punishment.
3. _____ Family mealtime was a pleasant occasion.
4. _____ Family mealtime was a tense occasion.
5. _____ When you were young, your parents forced
you to eat a certain amount of food or
certain types of food.
6. _____ In your religious upbringing, you experienced some form of fasting or deprivation.
7. _____ You were taught that some foods were
"good" and others were "bad."
8. _____ Some of your happiest memories happened around meals (e.g., birthday parties, romantic dinners, holiday celebrations,
etc.).
9. _____ You have received gifts of food from loved
ones.
10. _____ Your family often prepares and enjoys
foods that are part of your ethnic heritage.

Check the words that describe a meaning that you
have ascribed to food at some point in the past (either
food you give yourself, others, or that others have given
to you):

____ Love   ____ Sensual
____ Comfort   ____ Fun
____ Culture   ____ Gift
____ Sacrifice   ____ Generous
____ Reward   ____ Punishment
____ Warmth   ____ Bribe
____ Persuasion   ____ Payment
____ Satisfaction   ____ Control
____ Wealth   ____ Fear

How have you used food? Check those that apply:

1. _____ When you think about giving a gift, food is one of the things you consider.
2. _____ You enjoy cooking for friends and loved ones.
3. _____ It makes you feel good when people enjoy your cooking or gifts of food.
4. _____ You feel angry or insulted when people do not enjoy your cooking or refuse your offers of food.
5. _____ You prepare and serve food to others when they have not requested it.

Now, go back and reflect on your answers.

How would you describe the level of importance food has played in your life?

_____
_____

Overall, would you describe the influence of food in your life as being sinister or nurturing?

_____
_____

Have you consciously or unconsciously used food to get what you want from others? If you have, has the food made a difference?

_____
_____

During those times when you used food to satisfy a personal need, describe what you *really* wanted. Did food help you get it?

_____

_____

Food is often used for leverage with others or as an expression of love. I'm not suggesting that there's anything wrong with creating a fine table for friends or giving food as a gift. But let's be direct: If you want to express love, there are many ways to do it, and sometimes food gets in the way of your giving what is really needed.

As humans, we have a need that is every bit as great as food—the need to communicate. If you really love someone, sit down and listen to what that person has to say; don't hide behind gifts of food.

Food can be heavily charged in other ways, too. It can be used as an expression of control or manipulation ("I've done everything for you and what have you done for me?"). Or it can be a form of bribery ("Stop crying and Mother will give you a cookie.").

If you find that you use food in these ways, consciously attempt to make substitutions on occasions when food might be used. For example:

- Plan a social evening with a friend that does not involve drinks or dinner. See a movie, attend a concert, take a walk, go to a ball game, or simply have a conversation.

- Decide that every time you consider giving food as a gift, you will find a nonfood substitute. For example, if you bring a gift to your hostess, make it flowers or potpourri instead of a bottle of wine or dessert. When you visit a friend in the hospital, bring a book, magazines, music tapes, or stationery instead of fruit baskets or candy. During the holidays, give friends thoughtful mementoes instead of cookies—and so on.

- Don't allow others to use food in a controlling way. If someone tries to cajole you to eat or prepares food for you without your permission, feel free to say no and not feel guilty.

WEEK 4:
The Dieting Life

How great a role has dieting played in your life? Consider that now.

1. When you were a teenager, did you weigh more than you thought was attractive? ____Yes ____No

2. Which of the following events were associated with weight gain in your life?

____ Puberty
____ Illness
____ Surgery
____ Pregnancy
____ Marital problems
____ Moving away from home
____ Problems at work
____ Vacations
____ Money worries
____ Divorce
____ Death or loss of a loved one
____ Other (elaborate):_____
_____

3. At what age did you diet for the first time? _____

4. List (as best you can remember) the diet programs you have been on, then answer the questions below.

Year(s)	Program	How Long on Diet	Amount of Weight Loss	How Long Loss Was Maintained
_____	_____	_____	_____	_____

What pattern do you notice as you examine your dieting history?

_____

_____

If you started dieting as an adult, do you weigh more or less now than you did when you first began dieting?

_____

_____

How much do you think you would weigh if you had never dieted?

_____

_____

WEEK 5:
Weight and Love

How closely linked are your sexual attractiveness and your weight and shape? In our society, where the cultural ideal is to be thin, many people feel undesirable if they are overweight. Even when they receive evidence to the contrary, they believe that people with certain physical characteristics are more successful in love. Now, examine your own beliefs.

1. List the physical characteristics that you think make you most attractive sexually. (These can be characteristics you have or don't have.)

_____

_____

2. List the physical characteristics that you think make members of the opposite sex most appealing.

_____

_____

3. Consider your current relationship (or an important relationship in the past):

- What are the general characteristics that make your partner a person you love?

_____

_____

- What are the qualities you have that make you a person your partner loves?

_____

_____

4. Review your answers to the first three questions.

- For question 1, which of the qualities listed do you have?

_____

_____

- Would your partner agree with your list?

_____

_____

- For question 2, which of the qualities listed does your partner have?

_____

_____

- For question 3, did physical appearance show up on your list? If so, how important, on a scale of 1 to 10, do you believe it is to your partner?

_____

_____

- Did physical appearance show up on your list of qualities you love about your partner? If so, how important, on a scale of 1 to 10, is it to you?

_____

_____

It is wonderful to have another person in your life with whom you share important things. Intimacy with another human being is one of the great things in life. But consider this: If *weight* is high on the list of reasons you value your partner or your partner values you, something is wrong.

I'm all in favor of people taking whatever steps they want to improve their appearance—including losing weight. But if you are doing it because you believe it is the only way you can win the love of another person, this attitude will only erode your self-esteem.

While you are taking steps to improve yourself and your life, you might spend time thinking about your own and your partner's attitudes about love. Is this most important relationship in your life held captive by false cultural standards?

WEEK 6:
Your Quality of Life

In chapter 2, we talked about Cultural-Biological Dissonance—the establishment of cultural standards that are out of sync with biological "givens." One aspect of that dissonance is the tendency we have to use dieting or overeating to solve problems. When we do this, we are using a "solution" that is not designed to solve the problem. It is therefore ineffective. Think about it:

- If you have a problem with a long-standing relationship, why are you starving?

_____

_____

- If the problem is job pressure, why are you overeating?

_____

_____

Starvers and Stuffers have one thing in common: Both try to solve their problems with food. But starving and stuffing are impediments that prevent you from improving your life. They are not solutions. Take a few minutes to look beyond the issue of dieting to examine the quality of your life in general.

Mark the appropriate answers to the following questions, as they apply to your life right now.

1. How are you feeling in general?
   ____Very good
   ____Good
   ____Just okay
   ____Sometimes not good
   ____Most of the time not good

2. How often are you bothered by illness, aches, and pains?
   ____Often
   ____Sometimes
   ____Rarely
   ____Never

3. How active are you within the community and with relatives and friends?
   ____Very active
   ____Somewhat active
   ____Not very active
   ____Not active at all

4. How satisfied are you with your personal life?
   ____Very satisfied
   ____Mostly satisfied
   ____Sometimes satisfied
   ____Hardly ever satisfied
   ____Not satisfied

5. At work, how often do you have trouble performing your job?
   ____Often
   ____Sometimes
   ____Not very often
   ____Never

6. How satisfied are you with your sex life?
   ____Very satisfied
   ____Mostly satisfied
   ____Sometimes satisfied
   ____Not very satisfied
   ____Never satisfied

7. Do you feel healthy enough to participate in your usual activities?
   ____Yes, all the time
   ____Most of the time
   ____Sometimes
   ____Rarely
   ____Never

8. How often do you feel depressed or unhappy?
   ____Most of the time
   ____Often
   ____Sometimes
   ____Never

9. How much energy or vitality do you have?
   ____A great deal
   ____Enough to get by
   ____Less than you used to have
   ____Hardly any

10. How satisfied are you in your relationships with your spouse and family?
    ____Very satisfied
    ____Mostly satisfied
    ____Sometimes satisfied
    ____Rarely satisfied
    ____Never satisfied

Evaluate your answers. In which areas of your life are you very satisfied or satisfied most of the time? In which areas are you rarely or never satisfied?

_____
_____
_____
_____

In those areas where you are very satisfied or mostly satisfied, what do you need to do to remain that way?

_____
_____
_____
_____

In those areas where you are rarely or never satisfied, what do you need to do to become more satisfied?

_____
_____
_____
_____

How has your satisfaction or lack of satisfaction in certain areas been influenced by your weight? Be specific.

_____
_____
_____
_____

How have the first six weeks of this diet influenced your satisfaction in any of these areas? Describe.

_____
_____
_____
_____

Now, answer this question:

Assume you are going to live to be 80 years old. What will you take the most satisfaction in having achieved or experienced during your life?

When we reach the end of our lives, things fall into vivid perspective. How many people do you think would answer this question by saying, "The greatest achievement in my life was that I lost weight," or "I was thin"? It would be preposterous to come up with such an answer. As human beings, our deepest longings are for a much greater fulfillment.

During this diet, you have started to recover your perspective about the role weight and body shape play in your ability to achieve all the satisfaction you want out of life. You should feel greater freedom and a new sense of anticipation as you look ahead to the future.

TWELVE

Ask Doctor Callaway

Will drinking eight glasses of water a day help me avoid extreme water loss and the resulting water retention?

No. Water that you drink is simply excreted by the kidneys. It does not replace the water you've lost from within your cells. The only way to avoid extreme water loss is to eat enough complex carbohydrates to produce sufficient glucose for your brain and red blood cells. When your liver is forced to make sugar from stored glycogen or stored protein, water loss is inevitable.

Will combining certain foods at meals interfere with weight loss?

The popular notion that combining certain foods will slow your weight loss is not supported by current scientific evidence. This theory was dredged up from previous eras. Anti-food combining programs are designed to address the problem of dieter's boredom by proposing elaborate programs with supposedly new information. If you really examine the diets, however, you'll note that they are all extremely low in calories. The gimmick masks the fact that they are just new variations on the starvation theme.

Why not treat my low metabolic rate with "uppers"?

As you probably know, some "diet doctors" treat low metabolic rates by prescribing amphetamines and other

drugs that mimic NE, and with thyroid pills. At first
blush, this might seem a sensible solution. But these
medications can be dangerous and, ultimately, ineffective. Taking excess thyroid hormone increases the break-
down of protein, which leads to muscle wasting. And
amphetamines place a strain on the heart and increase
the risk of fatal heart attacks. If used long-term, amphetamines have a devastating effect on the brain and
mental functions, and can lead to addiction.

Even if they were not dangerous, amphetamines are
poor long-term diet aid. Eventually, your body devel-
ops a tolerance to them and they stop working. And as
soon as you stop taking them, you experience depression, food cravings, and extreme fatigue.

As tempting as it might be to consider the drug route
an easy way out of your dieting dilemma, don't do it.
These drugs are not safe. They create a false high, but
ultimately severe withdrawal sets in. Most medical societies have condemned their use.

*I don't feel hungry at breakfast. Do I really have to eat
when I don't feel hungry? Isn't it better to listen to my
"natural" signals?*

Your "natural" signals, as you call them, are actually
determined by your eating pattern. What you're hear-
ing now are the signals of a malfunctioning body clock.
Once you restore your normal metabolic rate, you will
begin to feel hungry when you get up in the morning.
In addition, you will be hungry at appropriate times
throughout the day, and will lose the urge to binge in
the evenings.

*Why must I completely eliminate alcohol? I've heard that
a glass of wine with dinner is actually good for me.*

Alcohol is one of the substances that sets off the urge to
binge. It is best left alone while you are getting your
metabolic rate back to normal. You should also con-

sider that one drink is 100 to 300 "empty" calories (calories that give you no nutritional benefits).

Will behavior modification techniques help me to stay on my diet?

For the Starver and Skipper, the major behavior modification is to eat three adequate meals every day. However, we have found that certain behavior modification techniques are useful in helping the Stuffer redirect external cues that influence eating patterns.

Richard B. Stuart, a leader in the study of behavior modification techniques for weight control, has devised a series of recommendations for shifting inappropriate cues. Stuart suggests that the behavior modification goals include Undesirable Cue Elimination/Suppression, and Desirable Cue Strengthening. His recommendations include:

Cue Elimination:
1. Eat in one room only.
2. Do nothing else while eating.
3. Make available proper foods only:
   (a) Shop from a list.
   (b) Shop only after a full meal.

Cue Suppression:
1. Have company while eating.
2. Prepare and serve small quantities.
3. Eat slowly.

Cue Strengthening:
1. Keep food/weight chart.
2. Experiment with attractive preparation of low-calorie foods.
3. Allow extra money for proper foods.

In his Cue Strengthening recommendations, Stuart includes what he calls "Accelerating Consequences," which enable dieting behavior to be considered in the context of overall positive life goals. These include the development of objectives and subgoals and the means for receiving positive feedback.

Behavior modification is useful only when it occurs within an ordinary situation. For example, if you were to go to a spa or eat only prepackaged food or a liquid diet formula, you would not be establishing any basis for long-term behavior change.

Behavior modification also involves the introduction of a reflective element in your everyday life. You need to think about what you are doing, evaluate the influence of various cues, and make choices about the signals to which you will listen.

Is it okay to use artificial sweeteners in my food or to drink diet sodas?

Studies conducted on the effects of artificial sweeteners have shown no evidence that they contribute to an overall reduction in calories or to weight loss. It appears that the calories simply get replaced by other foods. It has also been demonstrated that sweets (even artificial ones) stimulate an appetite for fats in some people. You're better off not using them while you're trying to gain control of your diet. And, as your tastes change, you will begin to appreciate the nuances of food and find that you don't want it to be as sweet as you once did.

I've been watching my diet and exercising, but I'm not losing weight. What could be my problem?

I know how frustrating it must be to work so hard and not be rewarded! The first thing you should determine is whether you are eating enough food every day and whether you are skipping meals. Next, evaluate the amount of exercise you are doing. Even with a higher calorie intake, you may suffer from water retention and other symptoms of a low metabolic rate if you are burning far more than you're eating every day. If you are doing everything correctly and can find no cause for your lack of progress, see your doctor. You may be suffering from a previously undetected thyroid imbalance or some other medical condition.

You should also take a realistic look at your body shape. Maybe you are "normal" for your genetic size and shape but are trying to reach an imagined ideal that is impossible for you to meet.

My daughter is 14 years old and she has gained some extra weight. Wouldn't it be easier for her to lose it now, while she can still do it easily?

Most adolescents gain weight during puberty. If they do not diet, they usually lose it by the end of their teen years. Unless your child is obese, putting her on a diet now is the worst thing you can do. Not only will you be reinforcing the negative cultural stereotypes about weight, but you will risk setting her up for a life on the yo-yo diet treadmill. The best thing you can do is to give her positive feedback about her growth as a woman. And you can also educate her in good nutrition and the value of physical exercise—without implying that she should be ashamed of being a little plump.

Ordinarily, I do not recommend putting children on weight-loss diets at all, unless they have medically diagnosed conditions related to obesity. Children grow at different rates, and a child who appears to be overweight today often shoots up in height tomorrow. I also believe that if there is a lot of pressure placed on a child to lose weight, he or she is more likely to develop an eating disorder later in life. It is much better to encourage children to form good nutritional habits by keeping healthful foods around the house, educating them about nutrition, and involving the entire family in exercise programs. Whatever you do, don't pass along to your children an obsession *you* might have about being thin!

What is your opinion of formula diets?

In certain circumstances, when a person is morbidly obese and needs to lose weight fast for health reasons, a formula diet may be indicated. However, it should *never* be undertaken without ongoing medical supervision. By "ongoing" I don't mean just an initial checkup; the patient should be followed very closely throughout the course of the diet. Liquid protein formulas should be used only for as long as the person's condition is really dangerous—not all the way to his or her weight-loss goal.

In my experience, the long-term success rate of formula diets has not been high. This is probably because they don't support a lifetime program of normal eating. Dieters don't experience how they should eat once they're back on solid foods. They either gain back the weight or become so obsessed with starving that they become anorexic or bulimic.

Is there such a thing as being addicted to food? Sometimes I seem to have uncontrollable cravings for certain foods.

There is no such thing as "food addiction," per se. But in the course of normal life, people do experience mild cravings for certain kinds of foods. These cravings are worsened when you go into a "deprivation mode." If you are eating enough calories, including enough complex carbohydrates, in three meals per day, your extreme cravings will disappear.

I've heard that eating certain types of food will actually increase energy and improve my mood. Is this true?

In a limited way. We've already discussed how the absence of carbohydrates adversely affects the production of the neurotransmitter norepinephrine, which controls energy and mood. And you've seen the depression-related side effects of low-calorie diets. But the current theories that *certain foods* will produce specific, controllable effects is not supported by any conclusive evidence. Furthermore, simplistic ideas such as "eat protein when you want energy and eat carbohydrates when you want to be calm" can be harmful since they tend to be taken literally by dieters. Don't waste your time on unproved theories. Concentrate on getting your metabolic rate back to normal. Once you do that, you'll have the results you're looking for.

What will happen if I cheat on my diet?

That depends on what *you* think will happen if you cheat on your diet. Part of the great mythology of dieting is that if you cheat, you are doomed to spin out of control. (That is, if you eat one cookie, you must finish the entire box since you have "broken" your diet.) The concept of cheating or not cheating actually makes it harder for you to lose weight and maintain the loss for a lifetime. My advice is to relax. Make the most of your diet, but don't let a small wrong turn become a major failure. Just pick up where you got sidetracked and continue with the diet. Whatever you do, don't try to compensate the next day by eating less food.

I'm a smoker, and I also suffer from a low metabolic rate. I've heard that stopping smoking decreases the metabolic rate further. Should I wait to stop until my metabolic rate is normal? I don't want to gain more weight.

The health consequences of smoking are so severe that I can't imagine a circumstance that would lead a doctor to advise against quitting. You would have to gain 70 pounds to make up for the health damages caused by smoking a pack a day.

Actually, this would be an excellent time to quit; a healthy, high-carbohydrate diet and regular physical exercise are now believed to help blunt the smoker's cravings. The decline in your metabolic rate when you first quit is about 10 percent, but it will level off within a couple of weeks.

I am in my right weight range and my waist/hip ratio is normal, but I still think I would look better if I lost about 10 pounds. Will it really hurt me to do this?

Not at all—*as long as you don't starve.* It's fine for you to lose a few pounds for cosmetic reasons. The problem occurs when you try to lose it overnight by eating too little food, or when you attempt to force your body into someone else's (a fashion model's) shape. You should examine your weight goal in the context of the rest of your life, and place it in perspective.

I can understand your point about how the cultural standards are out of sync. But what difference does it make that I know it's wrong if men still want women to be thin?

Let me suggest that perhaps you don't *want* a man who is attracted only to your *shape*. It's not really true that men, as a gender, prefer thin women. You learned that from magazines, television, and movies. Let me also suggest that we need not be victims of the cultural standards. *We* create them; we can change them. And the best way to begin is by refusing to let anyone question your worth, based on your body shape.

A Final Word

The works of nature must all be accounted good
—Cicero

Human diversity is a great gift of nature. Yet, we spend billions of dollars every year trying to achieve uniform body sizes and shapes, in keeping with what is considered fashionable.

Health and personal fulfillment are precious commodities. Yet, we inadvertently sabotage the very things we cherish when we judge our worth by such distorted standards.

I have seen thousands of men, women, and even children following this futile course. One of my personal goals is to encourage our society to begin shutting out the false messages and stop supporting the distortions; to appreciate, instead, the gift of our diversity; to pursue goals that really matter.

If you have been on the weight loss/weight gain treadmill, you know that it yields few lasting rewards. Mother Nature can't be fooled. If you reach for a false ideal, she'll place it out of your grasp. I hope the diet program outlined in this book will help you get off the treadmill, recover your well-being, and achieve a healthy and desirable weight. I guarantee that once you begin to reverse the trends that have defeated you in the past, your life will change dramatically for the better.

When this understanding really hits home, some people experience an emotional release. It's a powerful realization when you finally see the possibilities: You can achieve your goals. You can be "normal" again (or maybe for the first time). You can feel good and have energy to devote to the important things of life, including life's pleasures. You can have a body that's fit and healthy, and not be worried every time you take a bite of food.

I am encouraged by the examples of change that are already in full view. More and more of today's models and actresses are shaped like *women*. There is open opposition to discrimination against overweight people. And during the past two years, magazines and newspapers have been full of articles communicating the message that starvation diets are the wrong way to lose weight. Our First Lady, Barbara Bush, has made a public point of the fact that her value as a woman, a wife, a mother, a grandmother, and a public figure is not diminished by her size.

The time is right for change because, for the first time, we can prescribe treatment with confidence that it will work. The research and testing of recent decades has finally come together in a unified, effective approach. The health professionals are cooperating in efforts to educate the public, to warn against gimmicks, and to change for the better the ways our society treats its diet dilemmas.

In the near future, we will again view extreme leanness as emaciated and unattractive—no longer worthy of emulation. The change is already beginning to happen.

Cultural norms are made by you and me, ordinary people. We have the power to change them. With new understanding and skills, we can look forward to having more fulfillment in our lives. Better still, we can assure that our daughters and sons do not have to run on the same treadmill. Can you think of any better gift to give them?

Index

Recipe Index

ABOUT THE AUTHORS

One of the nation's leading experts in nutrition and weight control, C. WAYNE CALLAWAY, M.D., is the former director of the Center for Clinical Nutrition at the George Washington University Medical Center, and has held prominent positions with the Mayo Clinic, the U.S. Department of Health and Human Services, and the National Institutes of Health.

CATHERINE WHITNEY has coauthored *Life After Harry* with Virginia Graham, a practical guide for widows, and *Born to Please: An S-Step Recovery Plan for Women Who Love Controlling Men.*

Bantam's Best In Diet, Health And Nutrition

☐ 26326	All-In One Calorie Counter (rev)	$4.95/5.95 Canada
☐ 27245	Anxiety Disease	$4.95/5.95 Canada
☐ 25267	Brand-Name Nutrition Counter	$3.95/4.95 Canada
☐ 26886	Complete Scarsdale Medical Diet	$4.95/5.95 Canada
☐ 27775	Controlling Cholesterol	$4.95/5.95 Canada
☐ 28033	Getting Well Again	$4.95/6.50 Canada
☐ 27667	The Rotation Diet	$4.95/5.95 Canada
☐ 28508	T-Factor Diet	$4.95/5.95 Canada
☐ 27751	Yeast Syndrome	$4.95/6.50 Canada
☐ 34712	Asthma Handbook	$9.95/12.95 Canada
☐ 05771	Dr. Abravanel's Anti-Craving Weight Loss Diet	$18.95/23.95 Canada
☐ 34524	The Food Pharmacy	$9.95/12.95 Canada
☐ 34623	Healing Visualizations	$8.95/11.95 Canada
☐ 34618	Jane Brody's Good Food Book	$14.95/17.95 Canada
☐ 34721	Jane Brody's Nutrition (Updated)	$13.95/17.95 Canada
☐ 34350	Jean Carper's Total Nutrition	$12.95/15.95 Canada
☐ 34556	Minding The Body, Mending The Mind	$10.95/13.95 Canada
☐ 05395	Seasons Of The Mind	$18.95/23.95 Canada

We Deliver!
And So Do These Bestsellers.